CW01081919

59 GREEK STREET

HOME OF THE
THEATRE GIRLS' CLUB
SOHO, LONDON

APS BOOKS
YORKSHIRE

APS Books,
The Stables, Field Lane,
Aberford,
West Yorkshire
LS 25 3AE

APS Books is a subsidiary of
the APS Publications imprint

www.andrewsparke.com

Other books by Catherine Howe:

London Story 1848
Feargus O'Connor and Louisa Nisbett
Halifax 1842
Holyoake's Journey of 1842

To the Memory of Deborah Lavin

CONTENTS

PART I
1880-1914

1
The Building's Inspiration

For nearly one hundred years, from 1883 to the early 1980s, 59 Greek Street was a place for girls and women, first as the Soho Club & Home for Working Girls, then as the Theatre Girls' Club until 1971 when it became a refuge for homeless women. The Theatre Girls' Club, frequented by young dancers, singers and actors, occupied the building for more than fifty of those years and it is principally the story of those years which is told here.

The plot of land upon which 59 Greek Street stands has a history which long precedes its fame as a place for girls and women. Its next-door neighbours, No 60 and No 58 had been standing since the early 1700s, built when Greek Street was a genteel place on the edge of London with nothing to the north but Soho Square, the road to Oxford, fields and a windmill.[1] Upholsterer and tapestry-maker William Bradshaw, living and working at No 60 in the mid-1700s, raised a structure of dwelling house and warehousing where No 59 now stands. This first building, described as large and light, had throughout the early and mid-1800s been home to small manufacturers, the Westminster Jews' Free School and, after a time empty, Alsager Hay Hill's employment office which was affiliated to Henry Solly's Working Men's Clubs.[2] The latter is of especial interest to the early story of 59 Greek Street: Solly and Hill were leaders in the setting-up in 1869 of the London Charity Organisation Society which spread an international influence in the giving of aid to the poor, albeit based on the worthiness of the recipient.[3] The eighteenth century building at 59 Greek Street had a social heritage befitting the building which would later be raised for the benefit of Soho's working

3

girls and women. In its last years it was functioning as a *maison des estrange* for the poor and friendless men of Soho.[4]

The person behind the demolition of Bradshaw's building at 59 Greek Street and erection of its replacement in the early 1880s was Maude Alethea Stanley, fourth child, third daughter of Edward and Henrietta Stanley, Baron and Baroness Stanley of Alderley. When in London, the Stanleys lived in Westminster's Smith Square. They were a family of varied views. In matters of religion the parents were Anglican, one of their daughters, Rosalind, was a doubter bordering on atheist, one son a free-thinker, another, Henry, a convert to Islam, Algernon to Catholicism. Maude Stanley is said to have been low church.[5] The matriarch, Henrietta Stanley, was radical in some, not all, her views. She campaigned for the 'right of women to the highest culture hitherto reserved for men' in other words the proper education of women, and was instrumental in the founding of Girton College.[6] She did not, though, support votes for women whereas her daughter Rosalind Howard did. Maude Stanley's nephew Bertrand Russell, described the Stanleys as full of 'vigour, good health and good spirits.'[7] He was also daunted by them and felt more comfortable in the company of his father's family.

Maude Stanley planned the demolition of the old building at 59 Greek Street and erection of the new because she wanted to raise something suitable for a club and home for the working girls and young women of Soho. She was fifty years old, single, living with her indomitable mother at 40 Dover Street to where they had moved after Edward Stanley's death in 1869, and by the close of the 1870s was already an experienced and effective social worker. Henry Solly was of her social circle and it is possible that her philanthropic district visiting was inspired by his lead. It is also possible that she concentrated on Soho's Five Dials for her social work because her brother Algernon already worked there as a curate with St. Mary's Anglo-Catholic church.[8]   Some five thousand poverty-stricken men, women and children lived in the streets of the Five Dials which ran fan-like from the southern-end of Greek Street out towards the Seven Dials, another famously deprived area. This petite and refined woman, Maude Alethea Stanley, entered the back streets and courts of Soho's Five Dials district encouraging the boys she found there to come to school and the women to lead better lives.   Her decision to open a club for young local women in the early 1880s coincides with the demolition of the Five Dials to make way for the Shaftesbury Avenue and Charing Cross Road development.

Maude Stanley had already opened a club for girls in a building in Soho's Porter Street, and a coffee shop and diner at the Stanley Arms on Wardour Street, then a place of *bric-a-brac* shops and furniture warehouses. One winter's day in 1880, a roaming reporter from the *Birmingham Daily Post* witnessed 'an immense crowd of working men, women and children' pouring in at the Wardour Street coffee shop door 'all asking for the plate of hot sausage, or roast beef, or boiled mutton.' Maude Stanley allowed nothing stronger than ginger-beer on the premises 'and yet everyone seemed perfectly satisfied.'[9]

In the minds of many nineteenth century social reformers, dependence on alcohol was a leading cause of working-class poverty and brutalization. It was estimated that in the 1870s a staggering £1,364,000,000 had been spent on drink in Britain.[10]   What bred the alcoholism was not much considered. The clubs for men and boys which had sprung up across the country in recent years, in part thanks to Henry Solly's efforts, were about providing an alternative to the public house and the devilment of drink.

By the early 1880s, Maude Stanley's interest had turned exclusively to the welfare of women and girls. She intended her club and home on Greek Street to provide a safe and improving place for the girls and young women of Soho who worked in the factories and workshops there; women who, she believed, were vulnerable to moral degradation and dissipated living. 'No one' she wrote, 'can tell the difficulty there is in finding work for a woman who has lost her character.'[11] Maude Stanley sought to raise these women up but, though religious, she was not a proselytiser. If women were to be kept from 'toppling over the precipice to the abyss below' it would not, she wrote, 'be by putting religion forward first, [not] by severity, by exclusion of all amusements, called by some worldly pleasures.'[12] No, hers was social work, albeit of a moral tone.

And so, at the turn of 1880s, Maude Stanley set in motion the demolition of the buildings already standing at 59 Greek Street and the raising of the new for her girls' club. She called it the Soho Club & Home for Working Girls and made sure the name would be clear to see to anyone passing along Greek Street for it was inscribed in large lettering on the outer wall running between the first and second floor windows. This and the Westminster Jewish Girls' Club next door at No 60, were two of the first of their kind for girls and women. The building rose up across the way and a little down from Greek Street's post office and the House of Charity at 1 Greek Street, which stands on the boundary of Greek Street and Soho Square. No 59 was no mean project. The new building's frontage extended fifty-seven feet. It had cellars and four floors above.

A description of it from Westminster's Superintendent Architect in 1890 gives this: two cellars and a warehouse comprised the basement, the warehouse being 'in a different occupation' from the rest of the building and accessible to the street through gratings. On the ground floor were two very large rooms: the Gymnasium 32'6" x 17'0" towards the building's north end, and the Supper Room, 32'6" x 13'6" to the south. On the floor above was the Music Room covering a total area of 1,025 feet (and extending almost the

6

entire length of the building so clearly intended as a place for large gatherings and entertainments) and which could be divided into two parts by doors and shutters. In the Music Room was a moveable platform 16'x 8', which on the day of the Superintendent Architect's visit was pushed to the east side.[13]

The building had two staircases. The main staircase rose at the building's north end from the 5'9" hallway, entered from Greek Street through outer double doors. This sweeping staircase was made of stone spandrel steps 3'3" wide to its iron handrail and balusters. Its entire length ran from basement to second floor. The second staircase in the south-west angle of the building, accessible from the Music Room, descended by stone spandrel steps to a street door, but rose by steps of wood from the first floor up to the fourth. On the building's second floor were bedrooms and a milliners' work room. The third floor was given over entirely to bedrooms. The fourth floor also had bedrooms and a laundry and drying room.

The building was gas lit and heated from open fireplaces. Later descriptions suggest there was a good deal of wood panelling in the communal rooms. The Superintendent Architect does not mention bathrooms because there was none; 'we wish that there were space in London clubs to admit of such a convenience,' wrote Maude Stanley.[14] Nor is there mention of the morning sun which shone through the large windows facing Greek Street, and in the afternoons through the windows overlooking Bateman's Buildings at the rear. No 59 Greek Street enjoyed much natural light. This is the building, now reconstructed internally so that only its outer walls survive, which stands on the plot known as 59 Greek Street, built for Maude Stanley in 1883 and which was to become Virginia Compton's Theatre Girls' Club before the end of World War I.

2
The Soho Club & Home for Working Girls

During her time district visiting in the Five Dials, Maude Stanley had succeeded in encouraging some of her female protégés to live a more exemplary life, but she found that others viewed her home visits as intrusive. Her appearance at their doors could cause gossip among the neighbours.[15] There was a time when Britain's labouring people had thought they could drag themselves out of their dire condition alone, that socialism would prevail, but that had turned out to be an empty hope; the establishment held the cards and, slowly, was dealing them out. Nevertheless, the late 1800s was a time of national social awakening when greater effort was made, especially by religious bodies, to improve the lives of the working poor and to save souls. There was also, perhaps unconsciously, a feeling amongst the charity-giving governing classes that their position must be maintained through the improved moral standing of the deserving poor, for the governing classes had something to gain from correcting the lifestyle of those who served them. What is more, it was something purposeful which middle- and upper-class women could do in years when work was barred to them.

Maude Stanley was a general in this army of women. She had contacts across the Atlantic and beyond the English Channel. The lives of women of Maude Stanley's stamp were manifestly improving. Now you could study at Cambridge even if graduation remained closed to you, and the amended Married Women's Property Act of 1882, sent out the message that no woman could be regarded as a chattel – at least not in law. '[T]he ladies are now accepted everywhere, save in divinity,' observed one commentator.[16]

Maude Stanley had never, in any case, been prepared to be idle. Saving the poor was, in a sense, her own salvation; the building of 59 Greek Street would have been of great significance to her. She had raised funds and taken out loans amounting to some £2,000 for the purpose.

At this exact time, a philanthropic movement was taking place within the theatres, although of a different kind from those established by the likes of Henry Solly and Maude Stanley. Henry Irving (friend of Virginia Compton who would become the lessee of 59 Greek Street) together with four fellow theatre managers, John Lawrence Toole, Squire Bancroft, Wilson Barrett and William Hunter Kendal (Charles Wyndham could not attend) met on the evening of 4th May 1882 in the Beefsteak Room at the Lyceum Theatre and agreed that London's theatre managers should be asked to raise a fund for the relief of distressed actors, the fund to be called The Actors' Benevolent Fund. And so, just as Maude Stanley was preparing to open her Soho Club & Home for Working Girls on Greek Street, the Actors' Benevolent Fund was preparing from its office at 8 Adam Street to hold its first fund raising benefit at the Drury Lane Theatre Royal in aid of struggling actors, which it did on the afternoon of 28th May 1883. £700 was raised that day. Irving performed, as did thirty-six-year-old Ellen Terry.[17] Ellen Terry and others involved in the running of the Fund would give their time to Virginia Compton's Theatre Girls' Club when it moved to 59 Greek Street, but that would not be for another thirty-four years.

There was a well-attended ceremony for the inauguration of Maude Stanley's Soho Club & Home for Working Girls, held in the music room at the newly built 59 Greek Street. On the evening of Saturday, 3rd November 1883, Princess Christian of Schleswig-Holstein, fifth child of Queen Victoria, and suffering from a sore throat, declared the club open in the presence of a good crowd representing those from the legal, religious and aristocratic worlds. Maude Stanley arrived for the occasion in an omnibus from her home at 40 Dover Street, St George's. The club already had active members who had instituted a subscription to off-set the loan for building, and had prepared an evening concert for their guests.[18]

The Soho Club & Home for Working Girls would provide succour and activities to the local female community for the next thirty-five years. However, it was not a refuge for the homeless or hopeless; its rules stated that it provided lodgings for young women engaged in business.

> Rent of Bedroom, including use of Sitting-rooms, is, with Gas Fire, washing of Bed-linen and Towels, 3s and 4s a week paid in advance. Teachers or Students coming to London to pass Examinations can be lodged at 1s per night...Breakfast or Tea 21/2d.   Dinner 6d.   Supper 3d. Dressmakers and Needlewomen can be recommended from the Home to go out to work ladies' houses.   Entrance Fee to the Club, 1s. Subscription, 2s per quarter...A fine must be paid by members two weeks in arrears. No Member more than two weeks in arrears can be allowed the use of the Club. The Card of Membership will not be given until a visit has been paid to the Candidate's home by one of the Council. The badge is given after one year's membership. On Wednesday and Friday evenings, members may bring in a friend or their mothers to see the Club, on mentioning it first to the Superintendent.[19]

The badge of membership was a white metal brooch with a snowdrop on it, made in Birmingham. If you gave-up membership of the Club you would not be readmitted into the building, not even on social occasions with a friend; you could re-enter the building only if you meant to rejoin the club. Male friends were not allowed past the door at all, except for the Christmas party which ended at 10.30 pm. The destitute and hard-pressed of Soho never could have met a single one of the conditions laid out in the club's rules but any young, employed woman might, and she would benefit. The club served as a community, as a place of advancement; it was warm, clean, provided food, and it was safe in an unsafe world. Seven years from opening and the club had a membership of two-hundred-and-thirty, drawn from girls living locally, some as young as thirteen.[20]

Men and women of Maude Stanley's acquaintance gave evening classes and lectures to club members and lodgers. There were French classes, drama and singing classes, elocution and Bible classes, lessons in art and needlework, and music drills in the gymnasium involving parallel bars, jumping, and a ladder; exercises which Maude Stanley sometimes led, even as an elderly woman. They were 'such a capital chance' said one girl. But already the club had some notorious neighbours. 23 Greek Street was being kept as a brothel by one John Dearden. No 26 and No 38 were also thought to be disorderly houses. No 51, near-neighbour to the club, was investigated by the police and also found to be a brothel. Even closer, No 53 was a brothel. At No 56, three doors down from the club, Dora Biscoff was running an illegal betting club, frequented by the locals on their time off, and which eventually was raided by police at four o'clock one April afternoon in 1890.[21]

The greatest disturbance to the peace of the Soho Club and Home for Working Girls came from No 60, the grand building adjacent to the club which one-hundred-and-fifty years earlier had been home to the tapestry-maker William Bradshaw and then the painter Sir Thomas Lawrence. Now it was home to the popular Austro-Hungarian Club where cabs started arriving from ten-thirty each night, and where music and dancing went on until dawn.

Miss Ellis, the matron at No 59, was unlucky. Her room shared a wall with the Austro-Hungarian Club and she was getting no sleep at night.[22] Miss Ellis complained to the magistrates at Marlborough Street police courts and the Austro-Hungarian Club was raided by police at half-past-two one Sunday morning in June, 1886. The manager John Foster and club secretary Frederick Koch were charged with keeping a disorderly house.

By the time of the 1891 census, the Soho Club & Home for Working Girls, as well as providing activities for the women living and working in Soho, was home to thirty women, ages ranging from seventeen to fifty-eight, all single, two of them widows. At least half of these early lodgers had been born away from London and of these a good number were domestic servants, many were needlewomen, others went out as leather workers, boot machinists, bottle cap makers, jewel polishers, and all the other occupations local to Soho's streets. The club's matron, Miss Ellis had, by this time, been replaced by Mary Forwood, who appears to have had no live-in help to run the place.

Fifteen years later, Greek Street was described as the worst street in the West End. The man who said this, Metropolitan Police Inspector Francis McKay of C Division, stationed at Marlborough Street, felt moved to do so because many families had long been migrating in from the counties and, significant to McKay, immigrants from across the sea who over-crowded the buildings, commandeered the public houses and talked in different languages. By McKay's time a significant proportion, perhaps a majority of the population of Greek Street, was Italian, French, Danish, Spanish, Austrian, Swiss, Russian, Polish, Greek, Indian or Cuban. There were carpenters, warehousemen, book printers and compositors, coffee house keepers and restaurateurs, hoteliers and their staff, there were button makers, silver polishers, hat trimmers, dressmakers and tailors. Inspector McKay felt these people to be a threat. He went so far as to say that on Greek Street lived 'some of the vilest reptiles in London.'[23] Because of this he led regular police forays from Marlborough Street police station into Greek Street, especially on Saturday nights.

Close to midnight on Saturday 16th December 1905, McKay entered Greek Street with his men and encountered a group of German émigrés leaving Wedde's Hotel, thirty or so yards down from No 59 on the far side of the street. He ordered them to clear the street and one Ferdinand Altfuldisch, a tailor, was manhandled by McKay. The scuffle escalated into a running battle up Greek Street. The residents of the Soho Club & Home for Working Girls with beds at the front of the building would very likely have got up to watch the battling men on the night of 16th December 1905. The action passed right under their windows and on into Soho Square.

Ferdinand Altfuldisch, who was taken, under protest, to Marlborough Street police station, later accused McKay of assault and in 1906 McKay was called to appear before a Royal Commission enquiring into the incident. He had, he claimed, often seen Altfuldisch in the company of 'undesirables' who 'had an air of respectability,' which, he said, made his job difficult. The undesirables at the time of Altfuldisch's arrest were members of a club called the German Gardeners' Society. It was inferred that the German Gardeners' Society was a political club masquerading as a social club. Unfortunately for Inspector McKay, Greek Street's residents did not take kindly to being called West End's worst. At the close of the Royal Commission's enquiry of 1906, McKay was back-pedalling: assuring the Commission that he had not meant that the entire of Greek Street was the worst street in the West End, in fact 'there were many people there any country would be proud to have.'[24]

Maude Stanley was satisfied, that 'our girls...have but little [contact] with foreigners except when they find themselves as tailoresses in the same workroom.'[25] 59 Greek Street would, until the 1970s, exist as a tiny oasis of quiet respectability in Soho's square mile of brothels and drug dens which were tolerated by the artisan families living there and ignored as much as possible by the Club & Home for Working Girls.

3
A Woman's Place

On the surface, the function of Maude Stanley's Soho Club & Home for
Working Girls appears to be a simple source of safety and improvement to
its members and lodgers, but it went deeper than that. She and her fellows
of the property owning class shared a fear of what would happen if the lives
of the skilled and unskilled working classes continued to deteriorate. Society
depended upon the working masses to keep things running smoothly. The
strengthening of the fabric of society was her primary goal and the girls and
young women she nurtured were her darning thread.

Maude Stanley lived in a patriarchal world and she was of the current
mind that women were responsible for 'the good or evil in men's lives.'[26] She
understood that well-regulated patriarchies depend upon well-behaved men
of all classes, and she had come to believe that it was the moral fortitude of
her own sex which kept men up to the mark. Working girls and women were
necessarily 'at the root' to the question of 'how are we to improve the lives
of our working classes.' It fell upon the shoulders of girls and women to
somehow or other raise the moral standing of the men in their lives, in the
home and workplace. The lectures, craft lessons and exercise classes held at
Maude Stanley's Club & Home were the means towards training young
women to this task. The genesis of her belief went back a long way.

When she published her *Clubs for Working Girls* in 1890, Maude
Stanley emphasised over-population as the fundamental cause of the 'vice,
disease and crime' besetting working class districts. This over-population
was caused by the early marriages 'habitual amongst the poorest class of

workpeople.'[27] Too many children were being born to impoverished labouring couples and it was this which brought upon them 'conditions of disease and misery that must lower them in the social scale, and take from them all power of improvement.' This view of social conditions is no less than a repetition of Thomas Robert Malthus's influential fixed laws of nature which states that 'the constant tendency in all animated life is to increase beyond the nourishment prepared for it.'[28] This observation was to cause dire problems when left to be taken by Malthus to its ultimate conclusion.

In his *Essay on the Principle of Population,* published in 1798, Malthus rejected eighteenth century ideas of population increase as indicative of a healthy nation: a nation in which the blight of poverty and suffering was curable through the improved running of human institutions. 'I have read some of the speculations on the perfectibility of man and of society with great pleasure.' he wrote. 'I have been warmed and delighted with the enchanting picture which they hold forth, I ardently wish for such happy improvements. But I see great, and, to my understanding, unconquerable difficulties in the way to them'[29] These difficulties were set by a fixed law of nature to which all living things are subject: that our natural and proper inclination is to procreate but that 'The power of population is so superior to the power in the earth to produce subsistence for man, that premature death must in some shape or other visit the human race.' [30] It was not the entire human race which must suffer this fate. It was the poor, unable to buy the necessities of life, who would succumb to premature death because the great and pernicious problem resulting from Malthus's observation of natural law was not so much that he saw it as unavoidable but that he eruditely argued against acts of amelioration. To provide financial support to a poverty-stricken family was 'calculated to defeat the very purpose which it has in view' because it allowed struggling families to survive, procreate and so continue to outstrip food supply. The poor 'therefore in general must be more distressed.'[31]

By this truncated logic, remedial social intervention was an actual part of the problem. What was left, was the application of moral restraint by those who could not earn enough to feed their children. If this restraint were not applied, then the alternative was to accept that they, parent and child, would live and die horribly.[32] After its publication in 1798, great reliance was placed on Malthus's theorem by Britain's policy makers.

In the 1880s Maude Stanley was repeating this mantra. Lack of moral control, not lack of sufficient income, was the cause of working class impoverishment. As the wages earned by the working classes were, she rightly said, 'insufficient to bring up large families', moral control was the only solution to working class poverty.'[33] Malthus had also concluded that a greater social turmoil or a 'superior disgrace... attends a breach of chastity in the woman than in the man.'[34] Women bore the greater responsibility and the greater shame. Thus Maude Stanley felt it was of vital importance to educate young women to be exemplars of restraint in society; she saw it as every woman's role to 'improve and raise her generation to be something higher than mere hewers of wood and drawers of water.'[35] And here she is quoting from another influential social commentator of her day, John Ruskin, his lecture 'The Mystery Of Life and Its Arts'. That she quotes from Ruskin sheds further light on why she placed the responsibility for repairing a fractured and unwholesome society on her own sex.

John Ruskin's views on women, although well-intentioned, were delusional and fearfully prescriptive. For Ruskin, women are 'creatures born to be Love visible' and in order to fulfil their function 'must be incapable of error... enduringly, incorruptibly good.' He developed this notion by saying a man's 'soul's armour is never well set to the heart unless a woman's hand

17

has braced it' and went on to express its perfection in a sentence which might be used to sum up his entire philosophy on women: 'there is not a war in the world, nor an injustice, but you women are answerable for it; not in that you have provoked, but in that you have not hindered.'[36] Women are responsible for, guilty of every evil, while they fulfil their subservient role as help meet to the men in their lives. Many women, consciously or unconsciously, attempted to fill the role prescribed for them by Ruskin, and so colluded with his absolution of male failings and his fantastical expectations of females. Yet his message was a powerful and pervasive one, and his greatly admired writings and lectures of the mid-1800s, together with the ideas of Malthus on the consequences of an increasing population, give some idea of the source and inspiration of Maude Stanley's approach to her Soho Club & Home for Working Girls. In order to reverse society's deterioration women must be good so that men would not be tempted to be bad, they must 'ennoble the class to which they belong.'[37]

To compound the difficulty, this was not to be taken as an intention by Maude Stanley to elevate the labouring female above her social station. She was fond of a tale she had heard of a young west country woman whose 'voice was beautiful, and she had a natural talent for singing... the friendly kindness of the [local girls' club's] ladies caused her to come again and again, till the ladies arranged for her by her own wish to go into a home and to be trained for service.'[38] No, Maude Stanley's working girls and their male companions would, in reality, stay as hewers of wood and drawers of water. Yet, even though she was a devotee of Malthus and Ruskin, and although her young women were not to rise above their station or use their talents, she was not intellectually rigid. Intuition played its part in the making of her views. She understood the value of enjoyment of life, of dancing and singing and of how important these things were to the mental and physical wellbeing of young women. The practical work she did in the streets of Soho, in her Club & Home for Working Girls in its thirty-five years, brought a good deal of comfort, security and advantage to the working girls and young women of Soho: 'I say to my friends' wrote one 'that I should not know what to do with myself if there was not any club for me.'[39]

In the years running up to 1917 when Virginia Compton took over 59 Greek Street for her Theatre Girls' Club, Maude Stanley's Club & Home had achieved an air of greater refinement and comfort than the one it started out with. She would have viewed this as the proper and hoped-for result of her efforts. 'My girls of an evening are now reading Cecilia out loud,' she wrote to a friend.[40] The matron, now a woman called Florence Kemp, had five servants under her: a cook, a housemaid, second maid, between maid, and a kitchen maid. In 1911, the boarders were mainly in their twenties or thirties; four were in their forties, one in her fifties. Many made their livings from dressmaking or tailoring. But now, as the world rushed towards total war, there was also a compositor, stenographer, secretary, short-hand typist, governess, foreign correspondent, teacher of singing and a masseuse.[41] Within a remarkably short time, the trainee servants of the 1880s were being replaced by professional women of the early 1900s, all set to play their part in what was to come.

PART II
1914-1920

4

War and Religion

Maude Stanley died, suddenly, at her family home, Alderley Park in Cheshire, on 14th July 1915. She was eighty-two years old and had kept physically and mentally fit to the end of her life although friends had been worried to hear she was still leading the club's members in physical drill when well into her seventies. 'I was anxious about your heart, feared that the exercise was bad for you,' wrote one from Italy.[42] She left behind her the Union of Girls Clubs with a membership close to four thousand attached to thirty-five clubs, all grown from her Soho Club & Home for Working Girls at 59 Greek Street.[43]

It was probably late in 1916 that the actor Virginia Compton, now sixty-three-years-old, visited 'the house' as she would familiarly call 59 Greek Street once she had taken up a lease on the building for her Theatre Girls' Club. She had founded the Theatre Girls' Club late in 1914 and taken premises at 5 Little Portland Street early in 1915. In the spring of 1917 she moved the club from there to 59 Greek Street. The building was, of course, of perfect design and tradition. The Union of Girls' Clubs agreed to a 'very low rent' of £200 a year, on a renewable twenty-one year lease.[44]

Virginia Compton wanted the character of the Theatre Girls' Club to be 'that of a Home, leaving each individual free to follow her work and take her recreation so long as the comfort of her fellow members and the well-being of the house is considered.'[45] The emphasis would no longer be on sustaining a smooth-running society, more on the well-being of the young performers who came there. The hand-over of 59 Greek Street took place in 1917, by which time the country had endured nearly three years of war.

Britain had declared war on Germany on 14th August 1914 and on Austria-Hungary eighteen days later. British troops faced German for the first time at the Battle of Mons, on 23rd August 1914. Many of London's theatres were, by tradition, closed during August; the effect of the war upon acting professionals once the new season opened was awaited with anxiety.[46] Theatre-goers felt it inappropriate to be seen enjoying themselves so kept away during the autumn of 1914. Theatres went dark, tours were cancelled. In an effort to get in an audience, theatre managers lowered seat prices and their performers' wages to balance the books. This severely affected the working lives of young women working in chorus as dancers or singers. An uncorroborated story says that it was after seeing two young out-of-work female performers singing on a London street for their rent money that Virginia Compton decided she must do something to improve the lives of young women working in the theatre, and so it was now, in the opening months of World War I that she founded The Theatre Girls' Club.

Born Virginia Bateman in 1853, in New York, to American actors Sidney Frances Cowell and Hezekiah Linthicum Bateman, the future founder of the Theatre Girls' Club grew with theatre in her blood. Her parents took up the management of London's Lyceum Theatre in the 1870s and as a young woman Virginia Bateman worked as leading lady in the Compton Comedy Company before marrying the company's founder Edward Compton in 1882. She and Edward Compton spent the next thirty-five years touring the British provincial theatres. By 1914, Virginia Compton had long known that chorus performers rehearsed for no pay, that what pay they received when performing (a weekly £3 at very best in the early 1900s) barely met life's essentials, and she would know of chorus members in London's theatres fainting through lack of nourishment. For most of her life she would have witnessed at close quarters, even shared to some degree, the hard work and the hard lives of these women. A performer's life, she said, 'was spent in rehearsal on cold winter mornings, and at night putting on gorgeous costumes and throwing them off to resume her own worn-out garments in time to catch the last omnibus.' [47] Despite this, this life was considered preferable by many girls and young women to that of domestic service which in many cases was their only option.

From the start, the Theatre Girls' Club was backed by men and women of influence. Initial funding was secured through an early disbursement from Queen Alexandra's War Emergency Art Fund. Adeline Duchess of Bedford officiated at the club's opening at 5 Little Portland Street, on 23rd January 1915, and went on to sit on the club's management committee along with Herbert and Helen Beerbohm Tree, Florence Irving (Henry Irving's daughter-in-law), actors Madge Kendal, Mary Moore who had long been a supporter of the Actors' Benevolent Fund, George Alexander, Gerald du Maurier and Edward Talbot Bishop of Winchester.[48] Virginia Compton acted as the club's organising secretary while its first members embarked on war work by taking in orders from a company called Pineroyd, set up by Selina Gray, to make presents for servicemen on the front: water proof leather letter-cases or cases to hold pocket games.

The writer Sheridan Morley says that one of the first residents of the Theatre Girls' Club was sixteen-year-old Gertrude Lawrence who, by 1914, was already an experienced revue performer. Before the outbreak of war, she, as a fourteen- or fifteen-year old, had toured in revues with her father Arthur until he left England for South Africa at the start of war. Gertrude chose to find independent lodgings rather than return to her remaining family down in Clapham as she was determined to 'make good and 'standalone'.[49] There is, though, a problem with Sheridan Morley's belief that Lawrence's independent lodgings were 'the Theatrical Girls' Club in Greek Street.'[50] In 1914 the Virginia Compton's club had yet to move to Greek Street and Gertrude Lawrence says she stayed at The Theatrical Girls' Boarding House, nicknamed the "Cat's Home" and that it was a 'gaunt house in Charlotte Street.' Charlotte Street is a half-mile east of Little Portland Street. Howsoever it was, Gertrude Lawrence paints a good picture of life in this kind of establishment in 1914:

> Here, for ten shillings a week, you could luxuriate in a cubicle by yourself. For five shillings you shared a room with another girl. For half a crown you could have a cot in a dormitory. I never reached the ten-shilling private-cubicle stage...There was a great feeling of camaraderie at the Cats' Home. We girls loaned each other tram fares and clothes to look our best when seeking a job. There was a sewing room where we made our own clothes, and the stars of the London theaters [sic] used to send their discarded gowns to us to be raffled off at sixpence a ticket. I remember winning a pink net evening gown with a harem skirt and ornamented with beads. This I sent to Mother as a gift. She wrote saying it was beautiful and she was going to put it in a raffle! That pink net confection may still be going the rounds.'[51]

By 1914 there were many more clubs and associations for young working girls and women in London. On Dean Street in Soho was Lily Montagu's

West Central Jewish Club and Settlement; the Honor Club ran from 118 Great Titchfield Street; the Esperance Girls' Club was also north of Oxford Street, and specifically for theatre workers the two most prominent seem to have been the Rehearsal Club in Leicester Square, and the Three Arts Club founded by Lena Ashwell on the Marylebone Road.

As to women's political pressure groups, the trend at the start of war was to turn to supporting the war effort. Members of The Actresses' Franchise League, Ellen Terry, Decima and Eva Moore, Sybil Thorndyke, Gertrude Kingston, Lena Ashwell, participated in the formation of the Women's Emergency Corps intended to assist the war effort. Ellen Terry, now a woman in her sixties and a stalwart of Henry Irving's Actors' Benevolent Fund, was a friend of Virginia Compton. They had known each other from the time of the Batemans' tenure of the Lyceum Theatre in the 1870s, the place of Irving and Terry's early professional engagements. Ellen Terry and Sybil Thorndyke supported the Theatre Girls' Club throughout the years of the First World War and for some time after.

War-time London can hardly be better described than through Hall Caine's simply drawn picture: 'it is eleven o'clock...the theatres are emptying, the supper-rooms are filling, and London, with its lowered lights, is looking like old Cairo under its dark mantle of night, with the difference that taxis are hooting through the thoroughfares, and in the silence of some of the narrower streets, which flank the great railway stations, lines of ambulance wagons are waiting for their nightly toll of our wounded from the front.'[53] By this time the theatres were in full swing again It had been realised that entertainments were an essential release for soldiers from the intensity of war-making, a perfect way to salve heartache, boost endurance, bring brief forgetfulness. Also, entertainers were proving to be an invaluable source of fund-raising.

Actor Owen Nares, who later involved himself in the business of the Theatre Girls' Club, was an indefatigable war funds raiser. And so, despite the concerns at start of war, the theatres soon resurged – in fact they boomed.

West End entertainments may have been a relief to soldiers reeling from the horrors of the trenches but Arthur Winnington-Ingram, Bishop of London, was concerned at the increasing trend of servicemen visiting London to seek out prostitutes, the majority of whom, it was said, were infected with a venereal disease of one kind or another. Soho was a port-of-call for any man seeking a sexual encounter. The bishop criticised 'certain sketches and parts of revues produced at music halls and variety theatres,' and castigated the playwrights for their 'lecherous and… slimy plays' and of having the 'insolence to make money out of the weaknesses of our boys.'[54] He worked to abolish the promenades in London's music halls where initial encounters between soldier and female prostitute often took place. At the other end of the pole, one theatrical manager of a child troupe asked if military officers could not be prevented 'from waiting outside stage doors and stopping little girls in socks in the street.'[55]

The influx of servicemen into London produced a surge in venereal disease. For many, the solution was to control and withhold prostitutes from the men as the authorities had done back in the 1860s under the controversial Contagious Diseases Act. Hoary old tales of woman as temptress and harlot were profoundly ingrained in the national psyche: there is the Biblical temptress Eve, and the female from Revelation 17:6, 'drunken with the blood of the saints, and with the blood of the martyrs of Jesus.' On the streets of London it went both ways. The National Union of Women's Suffrage and the National Union of Women Workers secured permission from the Home Office and the Metropolitan Police Authority to form Women's Patrols –

vigilante groups in all but name – to protect vulnerable women from the sexual advances of soldiers.[56]

And so, Virginia Compton's endeavours to provide a safe place for young female theatrical performers in war-time London took place in an atmosphere heavy with anxiety over a society which was seen to be deteriorating: that same anxiety which had motivated Maude Stanley to found the Soho Club & Home thirty-five years earlier, only now the anxiety was accelerated by the effects of world war. When women swapped domestic work for work previously preserved for men now in the trenches, dread of abandonment of the purity of Britain's domestic way of life exercised many minds. In 1916 a Mission of Repentance and Hope was set up by Randall Davidson, Archbishop of Canterbury, in response to evidence that the war was lowering public morale and disturbing domestic norms.[57] A woman's place was in the house and everyone (excepting a good proportion of the female population) wanted her back there. Arthur Winnington-Ingram was the mission's chairman, and it is interesting to find Virginia Compton attending at least one of the mission's meetings. This poses the question, did Virginia Compton share to the same degree the anxieties raised by a changing society, and if she did, how did it affect her approach to the running of the Theatre Girls' Club?

Quite how Virginia Compton viewed herself in relation to her charges is difficult to assess for she did not write books about it as Maude Stanley did. Unlike Stanley's Club & Home for Working Girls which had catered for young employed women of a certain calibre, the Theatre Girls' Club's doors were open to all, employed or unemployed, so there lies one significant difference. A condition was attached to this for, according to her son Compton Mackenzie, Virginia Compton did not 'feel that we should put up indefinitely girls who are not doing any kind of work'[58] She is also reported to have said that the club was there 'for times of adversity and sickness and a place where [girls] may find a bed, a meal and a word of kindly cheer when they are "up against it", and to many of the girls it is the one place where the strength and inspiration of religion is brought into their lives.'[59]

This last is significant. Virginia Compton was a devout High Anglican and was familiar with those within the Church of England's hierarchy, which explains her appearance at a Mission of Repentance and Hope meeting in 1916. Compton Mackenzie often mentions his mother's Anglo-Catholic convictions in his autobiography.[60] One of the first things she did when taking over 59 Greek Street in 1917 was to ask Father Reginald Kingdon, minister at St John's on the Isle of Dogs, to take the club's first Lent course.[61] The chapel on the building's second floor, remembered by later boarders, was not mentioned back in 1870 by the visiting superintendent architect, so it is safe to say it was constructed by Virginia Compton for private services after her move to the building in 1917. And so from the start, she was bringing religious worship to the young women who stayed at the club.

Religious observance, it is safe to say, was an integral part of Virginia Compton's nurturing of boarders at the club. Both she and Maude Stanley were seeking to improve and protect but there are discernible differences between them. Maude Stanley, a Low Churchwoman, was concerned to preserve a society bound by rules learned from Christian Protestant traditions; Virginia Compton, as an Anglo-Catholic, seems to have wanted to bring a discipline to the young women in her care which would enrich their inner selves. Her charges were far closer in work and life to her than any had been to the aristocratic Maude Stanley, and despite the overt religiousness of the Theatre Girls' Club in its early years, and although it is perilous to adduce motive from interpretation of the evidence, it is reasonable to suggest that

Virginia Compton brought less moral judgement to her role than Maude Stanley, less by way of social engineering. She seems to have wanted to bring comfort.

The responsibility she felt for those who came to the club showed itself in practical ways. Boarders not doing well on the stage she would help to get jobs in another profession 'of their own choosing.'[62] And when in 1918 a troupe of dancers, recruited from the club, found themselves in Paris under a crooked impresario and ruthless landlord (suggesting some form of predatory coercion) it was to Virginia Compton they wrote for help. She promptly contacted the chaplain of the English church in Paris, Frederick Anstruther Cardew, on the Rue Auguste Vacquerie, who took the young dancers to the English Consul to ensure their safety.[63] Club members benefitted from this close contact with church establishment.

Interestingly, the Bishop of London, Arthur Winnington-Ingram, who so despised certain West End entertainments, was a great and lasting friend to the Theatre Girls' Club. He attended some club management meetings and paid visits to 59 Greek Street for as long as he lived.

An incident which hit the headlines in 1918 casts light on the Compton family's approach to life. The war produced not only a surge in venereal disease but also in drug-taking. Cocaine, until 1916, was advertised in Britain as a cure for minor ailments. It was sold in tablet form to sooth the throats of singers. Medical kits containing it were on sale. Harrods marketed it as a useful present to send to the troops at the front. By 1916, added to the horror of spreading venereal disease was now the horror of narcotics as their effect upon the troops became apparent. The Army Council banned supplies of cocaine to soldiers unless for medical purposes, while private dope parties continued at some expensive West End addresses.

In the spring of 1918, Virginia Compton's youngest daughter Fay, also an actor, was playing at the Prince of Wales Theatre along with her friend Billie Carleton. Fay was twenty-three years old, Billie Carleton twenty-two and starting out on her career as an actor and singer. Billie Carleton had developed a taste for cocaine. Soho, with its clubs and brothels was a prime area in which to find drug dealers. It was not, though, from the Soho or East End dealers that Billie Carleton got her drugs. Hers came from a young dress designer called Reggie de Veulle.

On the night of Wednesday 27 November 1918, two weeks after the signing of the Armistice, Billie Carleton and Fay Compton went together to a Victory Ball held at the Royal Albert Hall. They shared a private box and had a good time. In the early hours, Fay went with Billie to her flat on Long Acre along with other friends, then after breakfast left for her own home in Hereford Square. Billie Carleton must have taken the cocaine now, for she went to bed to sleep and never woke up.

And so, the young Fay Compton was caught-up in what had become, by 1918, the scandal of drug-taking. A photograph taken of her arm-in-arm and smiling with Billie Carleton and another actor, Lionel Belcher, was printed in the *News of the World* under the heading "West-End Dope Parties". Belcher was materially involved in the enquiry into Billie Carleton's death. The implication was that Fay Compton was involved too, and had been attending West End dope parties with her friends. To correct this impression, she brought legal proceedings against the paper. £100 damages were awarded to her by the King's Bench, all of which she gave towards the running of the Theatre Girls' Club.[64]

5

Daily Club Life, 1920s

In 1918 Virginia Compton incorporated the Theatre Girls' Club as a recognized charity'[65] There were now over two hundred registered members. Lodgers in work paid 21s 6d a week for bed and board, those who were unemployed paid 17s 6d. Although war was still being waged, the work with Pineroyd had ended with the change of location.[66] Within three years of this, boarders in work were paying 25 shillings a week for their bed and board, for those out of work it was £1. This is an increase of some 25 per cent on 1917 rates. Funding would always be a vexing matter to the club's managers, who relied upon income from investments.

And so began the 1920s, that remarkable decade which much like the 1960s would prove to be a transition from one set of societal norms to another. It became obvious that the women who had worked in wartime industries did not want to go back to their old lives. One member of parliament alerted his fellows to the fact that 'many girls who at present are in receipt of unemployment are refusing to return to domestic service.'[68] Employers began to hope that the offer of better wages and hours would be a sufficient incentive to bring women back into domestic work; cooks might be offered £30 per annum; house parlour-maids £22, between maids £15, plus full board and washing. Also, this army of female servants could have two hours daily to themselves as well as meal times, a weekly half-day off as well as on Sundays and two weeks' paid holiday each year. One employer thought 'such conditions would make the girl more the mistress than the employer herself.'

The war had given the working class female population not only experience of a style of life which they found considerably better than any they had previously known, but its end produced a determination in those financially better off to enjoy life to the full – to be carefree bright young things. A war like no other had been survived, a flu pandemic like no other in living memory had been survived, now life of a more liberated kind opened up its arms to the survivors. The new post-war woman 'was aiming at the enjoyment of herself (suitably encouraged by *avante-garde* males) of the same standards as men,' wrote historian Arthur Marwick in 1970.[70] More Soho nightclubs opened to cater for the restless bright young things: on Greek Street, The Harlequin and The African. 'Society thought they were slumming when they rolled from Curzon Street to Gerrard Street in their then modern Rolls Royces,' said a nascent gangster of the area with some contempt.[71] The less bright young things continued to work in the area's small manufactories and workshops, labouring on as before; a good many producing the lighter, looser dresses which replaced the corseted ankle length affairs that had constrained women until now.

Over in Berwick Street you could, for 10 shillings, buy an injection of cocaine in a cellar café courtesy of drug dealer and erstwhile actor Eddie Manning, and making their entrances onto the scene were gangsters who would become leading influences on Soho life in later decades: first the Sabini brothers, then Billy Hill, Bert Marsh and their underling Albert Dimes: young men flexing their early criminal muscles.[72]

Ellen Terry, who by the 1920s had appeared in her first film *Her Greatest Performance* produced by the Soho based Ideal Film Company, loyally supported the Theatre Girls' Club in the raising of funds which was an endless task. She attended the annual Lord Mayor's meeting at the Mansion House to discuss the club's affairs early in May 1920 and the following year a young Sybil Thorndyke took Terry's place.[73] Singers Clara Butt and Marie Tempest, the latter just returned from America, showed up for the 1923 meeting along with actor Owen Nares who had energetically helped raise funds for the war effort. Lilian Braithwaite, soon to play opposite Noel Coward in *The Vortex,* was there that day too. And the Bishop of London, Arthur Winnington-Ingram, continued to enjoy his visits to the club on Greek Street. He found it 'a much more jolly and lively club than the Athenaeum.'[74]

The bishop could not know that the police as well as independent watch-dog associations were keeping an eye on an establishment known as the Comfortable Restaurant three doors down from the club. This is the same building raided back in 1890 for illegal gambling under the proprietorship of Dora Biscoff. Anna Gadda was running things now, at 56 Greek Street. The suspicion was that Anna Gadda was using the premises for the illegal sale of alcohol and for prostitution. The police officer in charge of operations, Sergeant George Goddard, filed a report stating 'there is not a tittle of evidence that illegal sales of liquor are taking place therein.'[75] This report would be examined more closely five years later.

In the 1920s, Theatre Girls' Club staff included Miss Pemberton, cook and housekeeper, and Lalla Stanhope, night nurse. Virginia Compton chaired the club's committee meetings which sat once every four months. These committee meetings were, for some years, attended by Constance Eastwood, and Collette Brée, Virginia Compton's companion secretary. Funding for the Theatre Girls' Club was a constant battle despite loyal and well-connected supporters. In 1921 the club, in providing its service to young women, employed and unemployed, had run up a deficit of £214. By 1922 its financial liabilities had risen to £278.10.11. With finances in such poor shape, the Committee was driven to consider 'withdrawing money from investments' to keep the house afloat.'[76] Matters were not helped when a fire broke out in the cellar which spoiled some of the residents' baskets, probably containing dance items as the basement was used as a rehearsal room.

In 1923, of the thirty-seven club residents, four were in work and only one of these working in the theatre.[77] The club could not rely on payments from its boarders to keep it financially afloat and this was the ongoing trend. Fay Compton gave at least one fund raising concert at the club in 1923, and Sybil Thorndyke joined her for another concert in February playing alongside some of the boarders.[78] It is a great pity there are no archived descriptions of these events.

All this time, Virginia Compton kept arms-length from the day-to-day running of the club. Her son, Compton Mackenzie, said 'her imagination was no longer required to maintain the Theatre Girls' Club.'[79] Even so, the club ran very much along the lines she envisaged which was to offer a strong religious element. The priest Father Kingdon, who had led the Lent course of 1917, still came to No 59, and the Reverend Evelyn Kingsbury acted as the club's chaplain. Communion was held once a month, usually the last Wednesday of the month, in the chapel off the second-floor corridor, with its wooden seats and simple altar. Everyone attending the ceremonies had to wear a hat, and the officiating priest used Room 11, adjacent to the chapel, as a robing place. Some of the girls living at No 59 were confirmed in the chapel during these years.[80] There is no evidence of compulsion to attend religious service at the club on Greek Street but a religious ethos was certainly present. The expectation was there.

As Compton Mackenzie says, during the first half of the 1920s Virginia Compton was engaged in matters beyond those taking place at 59 Greek Street. From 1920 to 1923 she managed Nottingham's Grand Theatre where she installed the Compton Comedy Company in repertory. With a theatre staff of eighty, they opened on 20th September 1920 with *The School for Scandal* and after two full seasons had presented thirty-four different plays. They played at Nottingham for three years 'by the end of which,' Compton Mackenzie writes 'my mother had lost too much money to carry on. Nevertheless, later on she started a repertory theatre at Cheltenham and managed to lose a good deal more.'[81]

During an intensely hot spell of weather in 1923, at about the time the Compton Comedy Company was winding-up in Nottingham, small expenditure for the club was allowed. An annual payment of one guinea for a key to Soho Square garden was approved by the club's committee so that staff and residents could enjoy some air and shade. Also, the expense of a holy cross for the Chapel was met. The club's financial situation seemed to have continued upwardly in 1924 through a successful push to raise funds. One donation during this time was 'a very handsome present of crockery' from the Savoy Hotel.[82] Also the music room's grand piano was paid for, and the club was able to spend £170 to have electricity brought into the building. There was also talk of installing central heating 'which would be a wonderful improvement to the house during the winter months as it is bitterly cold.'[83] Three gas radiators were fixed in the passages although it was thought impossible to put them with safety in the cubicles where the residents slept.

At the close of 1924 Ethel Henry Bird was appointed as the club's warden at £50 per annum. Ethel Bird was a fine pianist and considered by the club's committee to be a 'thorough Anglo-Catholic... and very musical –

sings and teaches singing – and is of suitable age 50 – but young for her age.'[84] Then, in 1926, £400 worth of National War Bonds held by the club's committee were sold.[85] So having survived a financial low point in the early 1920s, the club was able by mid-decade to spend money on improvements and to continue to provide safety and succour to the ever changing forty or so young women who lodged there, even though the majority of residents during these years was unemployed.

In 1925, at the age of seventy-two, Virginia Compton fell ill with pneumonia and grew depressed. She was widowed, her children were grown and her life as an actor and theatre manager had come to a natural end. In her illness she had moved to a nursing home in Nevern Square, across from the old family home. The Nottingham and Cheltenham ventures had brought her and the entire Compton family to the brink of bankruptcy. 'I'm afraid I wasted a great deal of money at Nottingham,' she said to her son Edward Compton Mackenzie when he visited her, 'but I couldn't possibly have continued as Bode's partner.' (The Comptons had joined in partnership with the impresario Milton Bode back in 1898) 'I think it's time now I left this world.' 'No, it's not yet time. You can't desert the Theatre Girls' Club,' he responded, at which she put out her hand for him to grasp.[86] Quite when her London address became 59 Greek Street is hard to tell. It might have been soon after her husband's death in 1918 when the family house in Nevern Square was sold, or perhaps it was now, after her illness in 1925 but it was at the Theatre Girls' Club that Virginia Compton spent the last years of her life.

And so, Virginia Compton swapped the quiet respectability of addresses of the likes of Nevern Square, West Kensington, for a building full of girls and young women on a busy commercial street in an area notorious for its crime and prostitution, famous for its diverse and unconventional community. Life at the club would have provided her with companionship, occupation and her own private place of worship just a few steps away from her rooms. She took over room No 13 as her bedroom, No 11 as her living room, both on the second floor. Her living room, adjacent to the chapel, was described a decade later as a charming place of flowers and soft carpets, 'a bright fire burnt cosily...and [there were] many photographs of theatrical celebrities'.[87]

She was well looked after in the last years of her life, there at the Theatre Girls' Club. The staff timetable at 59 Greek Street revolved as much around her as it did the residents. At 7.45 each evening the Night Matron went up to the second floor to '[a]ttend to Mrs. Compton's bedroom, put out bath mat etc. bring down hot water bottle, thermos flask and water can.' 'The glass cloth for the drinking glasses is kept under the washstand. The other clean one is kept in the little blue cupboard.' Everyone's laundry was collected each Friday morning and Mrs Compton's bed was to be stripped only if she was out early, otherwise 'it must be done when she goes to take Prayers, or after Prayers.'[88] And there were more instructions:

> During dinner, put on kettle of water to boil ready for Mrs. Compton's bottle, [then] take up directly after and place under the blue cover folded over the foot of bed. Take out purple eiderdown from...between wardrobe and wall, and place on bed. At 6.30 take a cup of boiling water to Mrs. Compton in her office.[89]

Virginia Compton's companion secretary, Collette Brée, was free to pursue her own life each Saturday afternoon, so in her absence the remaining staff dealt with the special things to be done for Mrs Compton. Collette Brée was obviously seeing to a good many domestic jobs when on duty. Virginia Compton's breakfast was taken up to her each morning and once a week, her office was dusted and the Chapel cleaned; dust sheets were kept at the bottom of a cupboard in the Chapel. She was, then, enjoying the kind of life only women of a certain class could maintain.

In 1925, the one event which Virginia Compton had founded the Theatre Girls' Club to avoid overtook one of the club's boarders. On 5th August, a young woman a week or two into her stay at the club disappeared. Mildred Culley, known as Suzanne, twenty-one years old, had been touring with the Beauty Prize Company as a chorus girl before coming to London. She wrote a cheery letter to her parents on 24th July mentioning a man named John who had taken her for 'motor drives'.[90] After Suzanne Culley's disappearance her anguished mother spent days trailing through London trying to find her. After nearly six weeks missing, a woman dressed as a nurse knocked at the door of No 59 asking for Suzanne's clothing. She held up a piece of paper 'which looked as if it had been torn from a postcard... [and] was supposed to have been Miss Culley's authority for the handing over of her clothes...' When questioned, the woman's vague replies raised suspicion 'and we refused to give her Miss Culley's dressing case.'[91] The woman was sent away but two weeks later a search was made for her and again for Suzanne Culley who still was not found.

There is nothing to say Suzanne Culley was ever found. Danger to enterprising and trusting young women did not wait so much in notorious Greek Street as out in the sunny world where 'motor drives' seemed safe and attractive. What was termed the white slave trade, the trade in children and young women as sex merchandise, had been known of since 1885 when *Pall Mall Gazette*'s editor, W. T. Stead, martyred himself to the law by buying a child of thirteen to prove the ease of such a transaction. He was sentenced in the autumn of 1885 to three months in prison. His helper in the exposé, reformed prostitute Rebecca Jarret, was given a sentence twice as long.[92] In 1925 thoughts must have turned to the possibility of Suzanne Culley having been abducted for these purposes. The white slave trade was a tenacious threat. Forty years after Suzanne Culley's disappearance, young women dancers staying at the Theatre Girls' Club were still 'very aware of the threat of the "white slave trade," especially if working abroad.'[93]

The club also sometimes had to cope with run-away children. In 1926, the year following Suzanne Culley's disappearance, a fifteen-year-old named Kathleen Murphy came knocking at the front door asking for help. Kathleen Murphy said she had been put out to domestic service by her family but was unhappy and wanted a more interesting life. She hoped to work in the theatre. Virginia Compton wrote to the child's father after which she was sent back home and probably back into service. The lives and prospects of working girls and women had not much improved upon the bad days of the nineteenth century but by now there was a national pension scheme, enacted by parliament back in 1909 and which benefitted women as long as they were of good character, and national insurance for the poor in times of illness and unemployment. Also, in 1923 it had been made a little easier for women to instigate divorce proceedings. Wives could now petition for divorce on grounds of adultery where once they had had to prove that the adultery was aggravated by 'rape, sodomy, bigamy, incest, bestiality, cruelty or desertion for two years without reasonable cause.'[94] Small yet significant changes but for young girls like Kathleen Murphy, longing for employment more interesting than skivvying, such a life was still prescribed beyond escape.

Church and philanthropist continued to extend charity to those barely able to survive, the *quid pro quo* being temperance and rectitude. The well-connected, charitably-minded governing classes wished these qualities upon the mass of the disconnected and poverty stricken in order to maintain a smooth-running society. The theatrical community perhaps understood the situation better than most because the top of the profession had always worked closely with those at the bottom. Leading actors and theatre managers like Virginia Compton knew that social deprivation was not necessarily a concomitant of laziness, ignorance or lack of moral restraint but that low wages were.

The national government might be pressed to pass legislation intended toward social improvement, yet in the 1920s vigilante-style organisations, formed in the after-shock of Stead's 1885 exposé of grotesque sexual criminality, continued to monitor 'criminal vice and public immorality.'[95] Two prominent independent watch-dogs, formed in the 1880s, were the National Vigilance Association, doing 'street work and assisting girls and women', and the Jewish Association for the Protection of Women and Girls.[96] Greek Street was a place on which these organisations kept an eye.

In 1928, Isobel Hardy who had worked for the National Vigilance Association and was now an inspector of the London Council of Public Morality, and Isaac Sharp, investigative officer for the Jewish Association for the Protection of Women and Girls, gave evidence at the hearings at Bow Street magistrates' court into the behaviour of police officer George Goddard of Metropolitan Police C Division: the same officer who had exonerated the Comfortable Restaurant, run by Anna Gadda at 56 Greek Street, of immoral and illegal trading back in 1923. Goddard had vouched for Anna Gadda's establishment more than once since then, doing the same for another Greek Street club called Alexander's.[97] Isobel Hardy had watched women known by her to be prostitutes using the Comfortable Restaurant and had gone so far as to enter the ground-floor restaurant to ask for something to eat. 'It was a long time before it was precured,' she said. 'From my observation it seemed that it had been sent out for.' Isaac Sharp had seen 'as many as six couples go in within an hour...also one woman go in with two men within fifteen minutes.'[98] All this happening three doors down from the Theatre Girls' Club. In January 1929, Sergeant George Goddard was found guilty at the Old Bailey of having taken bribes for many years from a number of establishment owners in Soho, including Mrs Gadda of the Comfortable Restaurant at 56 Greek Street.[99]

The doors to 59 Greek Street were always locked against these goings-on, and the woman who would man those doors for many years was, by now, settling into her role as club secretary. Agnes Mair King Bell, a woman in her forties and always to be known as Miss Bell was, as early as 1926 mentioned in club papers for having taken six girls out for a picnic on the Whit Sunday Bank Holiday.[100] In succeeding decades Miss Bell grew to be the club's dominant force and is still remembered to this day by those who later stayed there.

As to the club's young women residents: some were attending Ninette de Valois' newly founded Academy of Choreographic Art, precursor to the Royal Ballet School. De Valois had danced in London's revues and music halls when younger and was now working in collaboration with Lilian Baylis, owner of the Old Vic, so the young dancers from the Theatre Girls' Club would make their way from north to south of the river for their classes at the Vic in Lambeth.[101] At the club itself, Thora Darsie, who had her own dance studios at Westbourne Grove, came to give free lessons.[102] It was these lessons which eighteen-year-old Gretchen Franklin attend in 1929. She came from her London home as the club's classes were open to non-boarders. This is the same Gretchen Franklin who went on to have an acting career of seventy years, culminating in her appearance as the character Ethel Skinner in East Enders in 2000.[103]

As well as inexpensive and secure lodgings, boarders enjoyed another benefit from their time at the Theatre Girls Club. If you fell ill, the club sent you away to Mapletoft, an establishment it ran at Clacton-on-Sea. Here you could recuperate but were given no choice when it came to religious observance; the first two rules of the house were: 'Everyone is expected to go in to Morning Prayers at 9.30' 'Everyone is expected to attend a Service on Sunday.'[104] Smoking was prohibited outside as well as inside the building. At Greek Street the Actors' Church Union was involved in 'At Home' sessions held each Friday to which residents could invite two friends. These events took place in the old music room, now called the club room, starting at four in the afternoon and ending at six. It was a weekly event and traditional amongst many women's clubs. The Soho Jewish Girls' Club across the road from the Theatre Girls' Club held similar events. At No 59, sandwiches and tea were on offer, dancing from five until six, and then the residents would do the washing-up and putting away. And every Saturday the clocks were wound. A man was allowed into the building for this purpose but he was not entirely trusted and was to be 'accompanied, so that the times tally throughout the house, and all clocks are seen to.'[105]

This gives some idea of the daily life and atmosphere of the Theatre Girls' Club in 1920s Soho. Personal discipline and improvement were a part of the club's offerings to its residents. Virginia Compton and staff living at 59 Greek Street were aware of the dangers which could overcome the innocent like Suzanne Culley while the private anguishes of myriad young girls, typified by the runaway Kathleen Murphy, were lived unacknowledged by history. But although some of their less salubrious neighbours were bribing corrupt police officers and were, themselves, the target of vigilante watch-dogs, these activities going on at such close-quarters to the Theatre Girls' Club did not seem to be a threat to its residents at all. The memories of those who stayed at the club tell, without exception, how safe they felt on the streets of Soho. This is an acknowledged phenomenon. Perhaps the female prostitutes in the area cast a covert eye over the girls of the club. There is later witness to this.

PART III
1930-1950

6
Years of Transition

In 1929, in the London home of actors May Whitty and Ben Webster, the British Actors' Equity Association was founded as a closed shop union. The Variety Artistes Federation had been running for twenty-two years as a much-needed union for revue and music hall performers. As early as 1907, only a few months after its inauguration, the Federation brought out on strike its four thousand members. Moss Empire ran the roost of theatres employing variety performers and paid the rank and file at best £3 a week. In January 1907, in response to Moss's reduced wages and increased performance times, the strike was called by the Federation, the response was significant and ended well for the performers two weeks later. [106]

And there were other changes ahead for variety performers. The resilient belief of many that music hall and revue performances were a source of human vice, that their popularity threatened the veneer of social proprieties, did not have the sway in the 1930s that it once had had. After the opening-up of society in the 1920s, variety theatre managers Laura Henderson and Vivian Van Damm were not to be stopped. Henderson and Van Damm opened their *Revudeville* shows at the Windmill Theatre on Windmill Street, Soho, in 1932. The nude in classical art was accepted by the cultured classes, so modern female nudes in classical poses should be accepted too. No-one could argue the point so the Windmill's static nude tableaux were allowed by the Lord Chamberlain censors' office. One might imagine that some of the Windmill performers would have stayed at the Theatre Girls' Club which was just five minutes' walk from the Windmill's stage door, but the official word is that none did.[107] The Windmill's performers were mainly young women with homes in London and without need of lodgings. However, Audrey Corr who stayed at the Theatre Girls' Club in the early 1960s, in the final days of the Windmill shows, remembers dancers there who she believed were working at the Windmill.[108]

The Windmill's *Revudeville* shows of the 1930s were, in a sense, the final chapter in the story of Maude Stanley's prescriptive world, where women were the chalice of a human purity which was to keep society in statis. Now young women in London were standing naked before audiences while retaining their standing in society. This was a liberation of sorts, a staging-post in the advance of a more realistic, a less hypocritical world. Women could now display their bodies to that ever willing audience if they chose to without being damned for it.

On Greek Street, restaurants were burgeoning. Rinaldi's serving Italian food, the Canton at No. 8 serving Chinese food, and George Gaudin's Le Bienvenue which had moved up to No. 48 and was now called L'Escargot because it was the first Soho restaurant to serve snails, which were kept in the building's basement for the purpose.[109] The gangster fraternity flourished too. Darby Sabini and his family were running an effective protection racket in London by the early 1930s.

The owner of 59 Greek Street was still the Council of the Soho Girls' Club Union, ascending from Maude Stanley's flagship Soho Club & Home for Working Girls and now functioning under the auspices of the Charity Commission. Rhoda Countess of Carlisle, wife of the late Maude Stanley's nephew Charles Howard, was a prominent member of the Council of Girls' Clubs Union and appears to have been the primary contact between it and the Theatre Girls' Club.[110] Sybil Thorndyke was another member of the Council of Girls' Clubs Union. Since 1917 the Theatre Girls' Club had leased 59 Greek Street from the Council on a twenty-one-year arrangement. It had always had to work hard to meet its financial obligations and from the start had expended much energy in fund-raising exercises. Fay Compton continued her efforts, and early in 1933 her brother-in-law, radio's first disc jockey Christopher Stone of the London Regional Home Service, broadcast an appeal for the club. Christopher Stone also edited Compton Mackenzie's magazine *Gramophone,* reflecting the great hopes of the emergence of recorded music.[111] The Theatre Girls' Club was very much a Compton family enterprise.

In 1933, Virginia Compton now eighty years old, still president of the Theatre Girls Club and clearly feeling her age and the weight of responsibility which came with ensuring the club's survival, sought to put the club on a firmer footing by buying 59 Greek Street. The Soho Girl's Club Union was contacted and responded in December 1933 through their solicitors Tamplin, Joseph, Ponsonby, Ryde & Flux:

> The Council of the Soho Girls' Club have had under consideration your suggestion that your Club should purchase its premises for the sum of £5,000. As I think you know, the Council of the Soho Girls' Club is unable to agree to any sale without the sanction of the Charity Commissioners. A Member of the Council has now seen the Charity Commissioner on the subject and I regret to inform you that the Charity Commissioners would not be willing to consent to a sale at the suggested price. I understand that the permission of the Charity Commissioners might possibly be obtained to a sale at a price of £7,000, which you will

remember is the price which was originally inserted in the Lease as that at which your Club had an option to buy.[112]

If the Theatre Girls' Club committee were to be thwarted in their plan to buy the building on Greek Street, then some other way must be found to place the club and its members on a more secure footing than was presently held.

The Theatre Girls' Club committee at this time comprised Hilda Russell of 86 Eccleston Square, SW1; Margaret Bull, 47 Ridgmount Gardens WC1; Constance Eastwood, 31 Chester Terrace SW1; Alice Maria Watson, 4 Devonshire House, Brondesbury, NW6; Cecil Alice Duckworth, 37 De Vere Gardens, W8; Edith Hermine Glover, 40 Mall Chambers, W8; and Virginia Compton. Miss Bell was committee secretary. When they met on 22nd October 1834 it was decided that the Theatre Girls' Club must become an incorporated society in order to give some protection to those running it against debt and other legal liabilities, and so, on 6th November 1935, the club was incorporated under the Companies Act of 1929 as an association named 'The Theatre Girls' Club'. The association was to 'take over from the present Trustees and Management all or any property, assets and liabilities of the society at present carried on at 59 Greek Street.' The company would be carried on by a president (fifty-year-old Compton Mackenzie now filled this role) and twelve vice-presidents.[113]

A year later, in the November of 1936, the Theatre Girls' Club Committee decided to close Maplecroft, the Clacton-on-Sea respite property.[114]

Four Soho women were murdered in the months of 1936 and 1937, all four said to be prostitutes. First Josephine Martin in Archer Street, then Marie

Jeanet Cotton in Lexington Street, Constance Hind in Old Compton Street and Elsie Torchon who had lived in Wardour Street. The murderer of Elsie Torchon was found and imprisoned but it seems that the other crimes were not solved. And it was in the mid-1930s that five brothers, Alfredo, Carmelo, Salvatore, Attilo and Eugenio Messina, gradually yet surely took over the running of Soho's sex and drugs businesses before buying up local property.[115]

In perfect contrast, the Theatre Girls' Club received a reporter from the *Coventry Evening Telegraph* in early April 1937 who was given a tour of the building by Miss Bell. The reporter was called Vera Webster.

> One of the most important rooms at 59 Greek Street, spacious and lofty, is fitted up as a laundry, where girls can do all their dainty laundering. I saw girls from the provinces just back from a "tour" washing their tights and silk stockings and all their pretty clothes, whistling gaily the while, looking so incongruous with their smart coiffures, their little high-heeled shoes, their carefully made-up complexions, and capable manipulation of diaphanous underwear.[116]

These two sentences give a vivid picture, yet despite having been written by a woman they are of that cheerfully condescending, vaguely voyeuristic style then used by many male journalists. It is a projection of the pervasive notion of 'the good girl'; the long shadow of the female cast by John Ruskin. Notwithstanding this, Vera Webster's article is an invaluable insight into one day in the life of the Theatre Girls' Club in the spring of 1937, and her descriptions of the building are as valuable, in between her ready use of adjectives.

59 Greek Street [is] a huge and wonderful old house with a capacity for every need... The different rooms are delightful, the club room itself is most artistic in wonderful pale orange and green colour. The restaurant too is equally attractive with its dainty tables and bright flowers... There is a fine practice room in the basement and when I made my visit an attractive young artist was tap-dancing to her own accompaniment on her xylophone... and continued in earnest rehearsal all on her own. [A] kindly friend presented the Club with an excellent gramophone, which is constantly in use for those who dance, or do their "daily dozen" to keep themselves fit, etc. .... Right away at the top of this high house is a room of sweet peace and utter quietude, a most delightful little Chapel where I am told many of the girls love to spend uninterrupted moments of serious reflection . . .

Vera Webster says that from the chapel she was 'ushered through an unexpected door into the tranquil presence' of Virginia Compton awaiting her in her private room. There was then, almost certainly, a connecting door between the chapel and Room 11. Virginia Compton told her visitor of the aims of the club:

These are to help those girls to take hold upon life in a right light, to become normal, useful, and not to live on a crest of a wave that may break at any moment to their own undoing; to realise also that life is a responsibility during which the meanest can achieve the noblest. [117]

These principles were spread through religious example to those staying at the club in the 1920s and 1930s. The nature of that example seems to have been mild and devotional. Virginia Compton was an Anglo-Catholic who does not leave an impression of rigid religiosity. The Compton children enjoyed a full and free social life unclouded by feelings of guilt. The club's future president, Compton Mackenzie, also a professing Anglo-Catholic and supporter of 'manners, morals, faith' was liberal in thought and deed, tending to 'exert pressure against old fashioned opinion.'[118]   He actively disliked puritanism: 'Bunyan' he wrote 'would certainly have put me into Vanity Fair and... I would just as certainly have pitched him into the Slough of Despond.'[119]   This says much about the Comptons' approach to their relationship with the boarders at the club.

It is impossible to know what the boarders made of their overt religious environment.   Confirmations continued in the chapel on the second floor until 1940 by which time Holy Communion services were being held every week instead of once a month. Virginia Compton was made very sad at the death of the Bishop of London, Arthur Winnington-Ingram, in May 1939. He had been what she called the club's patron visitor from the start. And Father Reginald Kingdon, who had taken the first Lent course in 1917, was too ill to visit again: 'now it is over and it is a very real grief,' she wrote.[120]

On 3rd September 1939, Britain declared war on Germany for a second time in twenty-five years. This brought a good deal of anxiety to the eighty-five-year-old Virginia Compton who was incapacitated by her age and needed help to get about. 'Again, I come like the birds every Spring –' she wrote for the club report of that year, 'only I am much more like a dilapidated old crow – to pick up all the necessaries for my nest.' 1939 had been a strange year, she wrote,

> ...full of anxiety, great strain and astonishing surprises. We all expected to be demolished in September. Like every one else will have wondered why we were not...I don't think we could have been more "blacked out" than we have been – and yet even we have been visited by the Police to let us know that a refractory glimmer of light was showing. We instantly put more black-out on. We have made every effort to keep to our ordinary course of life as much as possible, and our motto has been "business as usual" – though we have not had nearly as many girls. They come and go more, also many have got war work of various kinds.[121]

Virginia Compton's thoughts were a little darker than might be apparent. She was afraid of the consequences should she, as the club's president, be killed alongside the club's treasurer in the Luftwaffe bombardment which most people seemed to know was coming. If they were killed, how would the Theatre Girls' Club carry on? And what would happen financially if the building itself were blown up? Miss Bell was dispatched to 11 Grey's Inn Square, to the offices of the club's solicitors Colyer and Colyer, to bring back assurances that the club's Memorandum and Articles provided for the election of a new president to take 'your place as well as another Treasurer' in the event of death. 'If as was suggested the Club itself was blown up then the question would be whether the Government would give any compensation for loss in the circumstances but the Society would go on in the ordinary way as the investments would still be in existence.'[122]

On 25th December the building's owners, the Council of the Soho Working Girls' Club, granted a further 21-year lease to the club at £250 per annum.[123]

7
Memories from the 1940s

A birthday party was held for Virginia Compton in the club room at 59 Greek Street on 1st January 1940. Everyone in the building attended and 'as it was a Sunday, a good many friends who cannot come on a week day were able to be there – and we certainly had a remarkably successful party' wrote Compton Mackenzie

Quite a number of our very young friends were with us, two or three in arms (no crying heard!). Mrs Compton's great-grandson, Alan Howard, aged eighteen months, was perhaps the star of the occasion – although John Valentine, her grandson aged thirteen, ran him rather hard. He and our own girls gave the entire entertainment which was really delightful, and very clever. The eighty-six candles on the huge cake were blown out, with great care, precision and much delight by the little children. Mrs Compton received so many flowers, telegrams, and good wishes...that she really thought she couldn't be quite as old as she was – it was perhaps the very nicest party we have ever had. We sang Auld Lang Syne, and then Mrs Compton mounted her chair and was carried upstairs again amid the singing of 'She's a Jolly Good Fellow'. The memory of this party fraught with happiness undoubtedly helped us in the later troubles of the year.' [124]

The later troubles, namely the Blitz, came in September 1940 but Virginia Compton did not have to endure this horror as her life came to its end five months after her birthday, on Sunday 5th May, in her room at The Theatre Girls' Club, and four months before the Luftwaffe's first visit of real devastation to London. She had been widowed for twenty-two years and had lived fifteen or more of those years at 59 Greek Street, within the community of the Theatre Girls' Club which she had founded on the threshold of the First World War. The impression is that she had prayed every day in her chapel on the second floor and had made 'the house' a house of religion under the wing of the Anglican Church. A memorial service was held four days after her death at All Saints Church on Margaret Street.[125]

The Theatre Girls' Club and the family life of the Comptons were so closely tied that with Virginia Compton's death came a doubt over the club's future. Change of premises was considered but not acted upon.[126] The atmosphere in the club changed after Virginia Compton's death for it brought in the era of Agnes Mair King Bell, whose managerial hand was applied strongly and remembered keenly. Miss Bell had been a staunch support to her employer and to the club for fifteen years or more. She had long acted as the club's secretary and would preside over its fortunes for twenty years more. Here was a woman for whom the Theatre Girls' Club was completely her life.

For the next twenty years, Agnes Bell's private rooms at 59 Greek Street were on the second floor (surely Virginia Compton's old rooms) and along the corridor lived her second-in-command Jackie, whose other names are presently unknown.[127] Miss Bell had been born in the Kelvin district of Glasgow in 1884. She was the daughter of a prosperous cigar and snuff manufacturer, Robert Chalmers Bell, whose own father, Finlay, had been a founder of Glasgow tobacco manufacturers J & F Bell Ltd. When Agnes Bell was a small child, her mother had died and her father remarried in 1893 to Jessie Gemmell from Ayr. Perhaps the sixteen-year-old Agnes Bell from Scotland attending Millburn House School in Lewisham in 1901, a boarding school for young ladies, is our Agnes Bell. Certainly, her father Robert was living in London ten years later, at 17 Bark Place, Bayswater, and we know that by the mid-1920s Agnes Bell, a woman by then in her early forties, was involved in the running of the Theatre Girls' Club.[128] She, as club secretary, together with Compton Mackenzie as the club's president, steered the house through the war years.

At the start of the war, stage work went on much as usual, 'girls were coming and going all the time' wrote Compton Mackenzie. With bombing from the Luftwaffe expected, Westminster Council, early in 1940, re-enforced part of the basement at No 59 as a bomb shelter for residents and for the use of other young local women.[129] The degree of bombing could not, at that time, have been imagined. The Blitz came on 7th September 1940 and went on until May of the next year. On 24th September 1940, seventeen days into this unparalleled bombing campaign, the two hundred and fifty-year-old church of St Anne's, two streets west of Greek Street, was demolished by a Luftwaffe bomb, 24 Greek Street was as good as demolished on the 11th October and later the House of Charity, across the road from the club, 'escaped destruction by a few feet.'[130] The bomb shelter at 59 Greek Street was used a good deal, Compton Mackenzie recorded.[131]

The club's fire precautions had to satisfy the local Air Raid Precautions Department at Alhambra House on Charing Cross Road. The building had not, in all respects, met Westminster Council's fire safety regulations back in 1890 but had not been required to make changes.[132] Any improvements to fire safety made since 1890 seem to have satisfied the ARP because the club's work went on unhindered – with one or two exceptions.

Three weeks into the Blitz, 2nd October 1940, with bombs falling, a letter was sent to Lady Carlisle at Bolton Hall, Gosforth, (an unsigned copy of an original almost certainly dictated by Compton Mackenzie, maybe typed by Agnes Bell or Jackie):

> I am enclosing a cheque for our rent £72. After discussion with our Chairwoman and our Hon. Secretary we feel that the Club should close down – only temporarily we hope. We have had a time bomb, incendiary bombs etc. quite near and the dining-room, kitchen and some of the Club room windows have been broken. The girls are not coming to town, and London for the time being is no longer the hub of the profession. There are only five girls here, and three of them are leaving at the end of the week and the other two are doing office work so can arrange to live elsewhere. We wondered, therefore, if you would very kindly consider reducing our rent for as long as we are not using the building – you have always been so very kind and generous to us that we do not like asking you to do this, but as we can only rely on the money from our investments coming in it would be difficult for us to manage otherwise. We shall try to get a reduction of our rates. I shall, of course, come in during the week to attend to correspondence etc. and should there be a demand for the Club, we will re-open at once.[133]

Lady Carlisle did reduce the club's rent early the following year but by then there were eight residents at No 59, so closure did not last long and, apart from a later short shut-down, the Theatre Girls' Club functioned normally throughout the war.

For many of its neighbours the story was different. Soho's cosmopolitan community was deeply affected from the start of the conflict. In London, nationalists, aping Nazi attacks on Jewish businesses, attacked German and Italian properties on London's streets and there were many German and Italian families living in the streets of Soho. The Italian coffee houses were said to disappear: that by close of war Soho was 'coffee-less'[134] One Soho Italian, Fortunato Picchi, deputy manager of the Savoy restaurant, was interned on the Isle of Wight when Italy sided with Hitler's Germany until he volunteered to be an interpreter and guide to the men of Operation Colossus who parachuted into southern Italy in February 1941. All were captured and Picchi was shot as a traitor by the Italians at Fort Bravetta in Rome on 6th April 1941. He was not forgotten by Soho.[135]

In these dark times, the dark side of Soho life went on uninterrupted. The district's children were as vulnerable as ever they were to neglect and abuse. A boy named Harry Alfred Cohen led a Soho boys' gang, putting on 'the airs of an underworld boss' perhaps in emulation of local gangster Jack Spot, until he was arrested for the theft of £45 worth of second-hand clothing. He 'looked tired' at his hearing in March 1941 and hoped the authorities would 'send him to sea' for his punishment but he was sent to Borstal.[136] The real criminals did well from black marketeering and continued in their violent ways. Harry 'Scarface' Distleman was fatally stabbed by Tony Mancini, night club manager of Wardour Street's Palm Beach Bottle Party in May 1941, and the proprietor of Soho's Havana Club was charged with the assault of a nine-year-old girl.[137]

The residents of the Theatre Girls' Club would hear of the tragedy and violence going on so close around them. In Wardour Street, on 10th February 1842, the body of Nita Ward, described as an ex-actress, was found by one of her neighbours. The killer was 'a sexual maniac' according to newspaper reports and her estranged husband told police his wife 'was fascinated by West End life and would not leave it.'[138]   The Theatre Girls' Club's front doors were securely locked against all these dangers. Miss Bell had the keys to those front doors and continued to ensured no-one passed the threshold who was a stranger and male.

The club had an unexpected windfall in 1942 when the Rehearsal Club in Leicester Square, established in 1892 for the respite of chorus girls and bit-part players, was dissolved and its remaining funds distributed amongst similar organisations through the Westminster Banks' Trustee Department. The Theatre Girls' Club received a disbursement of £400.[139]   With the permanent closure of the Rehearsal Club, young performers had one club less to turn to but another, the Interval Club, was already running from premises on Dean Street to fill the gap. The Interval Club was that unusual thing: a mixed residential club and this would appeal to a good many young women in the 1940s.

By 1943, some performers from the Theatre Girls' Club were working abroad with E.N.S.A., the Entertainments National Service Association. They wrote to the club from India, Palestine, Egypt.   There seems to have been a true emotional attachment between resident and club management at this time. One mother wrote to the board of trustees:

I should like you to know how much I appreciated your kindness to my daughter Evelyn while she stayed at your place in London. It makes such a difference to us here to

63

know that she can go to a place like you have and that there
is someone there who takes a personal interest in her when
she is so far from her own home [140]

E.N.S.A. was set up at the start of war by Basil Dean and Leslie
Henson to entertain the troops at home and abroad. Anyone who could dance
and sing, and was brave enough to board plane or ship travelling to war zones,
was essential to its success. Some Theatre Girls' Club performers were
torpedoed while sailing with E.N.S.A. All survived.[141]

The lives of most young women had always been exacting and,
although they were emerging into a more liberated and interesting world,
unashamed gender discrimination was still fully functioning. An example to
reach public notice occurred two streets from the Theatre Girls' Club in Soho
in November 1943, when Land Army workers were refused admittance into
the Nuffield Forces Club on Wardour Street. War Minister Sir James Grigg's
reaction was to ask: why were the women in Soho at all? There was 'no
ploughing in the street of film companies...no corn threshers.'[142] Six years
later, Simone de Beauvoir wrote with some restraint: 'The social structure
has not been much modified by the changes in woman's condition; this world,
always belonging to men, still retains the form they have given it.'[143] But the
idea of a more liberated and assertive kind of woman was implanted in the
national mind and ideas, howsoever long it takes them, do eventually bring
change.

Bombing started again in February 1944 'some of which fell very near our
house,' wrote Compton Mackenzie.

Most of the girls at the time were very young and did not
appear to realize the danger, and perhaps even enjoyed the

excitement. Only one or two of the girls went to the shelter... the rest seemed to feel safer sitting on the stone stairs. The flying bombs did affect the theatres adversely and sent most of the girls to the provinces... For this reason, we decided to close the Club for a month or so in order to give our small staff their annual holiday. There was always, of course, someone in the house, and one day when two very tired and very young dancers arrived at our door, having hunted in vain in the suburbs for rooms... we decided we must re-open and gradually, in spite of the flying bombs and rockets, we were full again.[144]

The 1940s is also the decade when life at The Theatre Girls' Club falls within living memory. By 1944 the club was sometimes revisited by old boarders, some married and with children, while new residents were, as ever, 'very young – many still in their teens.' 'We feel it is important' said Compton Mackenzie, 'that they should be as well fed as possible which we find can still be managed in spite of rationing.'[145] This was wishful thinking as the recollections of the young women who stayed at the Theatre Girls' Club in the immediate post-war years show. Reactions to life at the club are mixed but largely positive and one constant is that everyone staying there felt safe in Soho despite the nearness of criminal characters and frequency of murders disproportionate to the size of Soho's area.

And so, to the living memories of some who stayed at the Theatre Girls' Club.[146]

Audrey Crockett *(from Shrewsbury, stayed at the club 1944, aged 14)*

Prior to coming to London to seek fame and fortune I was a

weekly boarder at a convent school in Chester. I didn't do much in the way of lessons and spent each day at the Irene Hammond School of Dance. I managed to get an audition with Ninette de Valois to see if she would accept me as a pupil at the Sadler's Well Ballet School (before it became the Royal Ballet School), and joyfully, was accepted. I was 14, which then was school-leaving age. The year was 1944.

How we got to hear of the Theatre Girls' Club I have no idea. Mum was always supportive, Dad less so but I think that was probably from a financial point of view. Mum brought me down to London but unfortunately coming down the [club's] stairs, which were very dark due to the black-out regulations, to leave and get her train back home, she fell and broke a bone in her shoulder. Olive who lived there was despatched with me to take Mum to hospital – the Middlesex which wasn't too far away – where she was kept in, and according to my diary it was 11.39 pm before Olive and I got back to the Club. Who Olive was I am not sure but I think that she worked in an office rather than the theatre.

I have no idea who showed me around or anything about the rules, but I seem to think they were pinned up on a board someplace. There was a row of cubicles behind the sidewall of the main sitting/club room, the partitions were solid, not curtains, and I was in one of these. The problem is I don't remember windows, anywhere. They would have been all done up with that sticky stuff and heavily curtained for the blackout. A couple of times on later stays at the Club I was in room 7 and once in room 8. One of them at least was a double room and they were a big improvement on the cubicles. For me at the age of 14 it was the ideal place to be. And in later years digs in London were hard to find, so I think on a short term stay it was ideal; certainly for rehearsal periods.

I spent a lot of time with Mavis, Ann and Eunice, but have no idea of their surnames. I think Eunice was a soubrette and in ENSA, and I kept Mavis company when she went for her ENSA audition which she got, so they must both have been at least 17 or 18. There was a Catherine, Madeleine, Elizabeth Gammond who had been at dancing school with me in Chester, but was a bit older, and Audrey Hardy who used to tell our fortunes. I only had class in the morning – I caught the bus in Charing Cross Road to the Sadler's Wells Theatre. I spent a lot of time going to Sammy's for a cup of tea in the afternoon (no idea where that was) or going to the pictures.

I was never worried about walking around Soho or remember getting hassled. I do remember being pulled into a doorway when a VI engine stopped and waiting for it to fall. I don't remember an air raid shelter in the Theatre Girls' Club or any instructions for when the sirens went; though with the buzz bombs, when their engine stopped there wouldn't have been time to do anything. My diary records that when having a bath on one occasion at the Club a V1 stopped and I was scared. It also records that a number of times when wanting a bath the water was cold.

Miss Bell was in charge. Her office was on a half-landing, where the main stairs turn around, and she had a small dog which we called Bandy Bell. Miss Bell was very much like a headmistress or Reverend Mother in my eyes, but always very pleasant. One afternoon she came in the sitting/club room with another lady and I stood up automatically as I would have done at the convent. The other girls were cross with me. However, later I was summoned to Miss Bell's room and invited to afternoon tea for showing courtesy to her guest. The other lady had been Fay Compton, the well-known English actress who was, I think, a trustee, as was her brother, the author Compton Mackenzie.

I have a feeling that Madeleine helped me get my first job in pantomime – Babes in the Wood at the Memorial Theatre, Stratford-upon-Avon, produced by Harry Benet, salary £5 a week, which was more than the average. I also think it was Madeleine who took me to buy necessary make-up and taught me how to apply it. I think that she was also known as Scottie. I hope that I thanked her. I stayed at the Club the following summer [1945] while rehearsing for Harry Benet's Royal Majestic Circus – a very different experience from both the Sadler's Wells Ballet School and panto at Stratford-upon-Avon.

The following year I was touring in a revue, produced by George and Alfred Black, sons of the pre-war West End impresario George Black, and we kept going back to Scandinavia which I really enjoyed. There were 8 Showgirls, 4 ballet dancers, and 6 other (non-pointe) dancers. I was chosen for the ballet girls and as such was employed by Dixtra Enterprises. After that, in 1947 I did panto followed by a tour with Harry Benet again in the Walt Disney version of Snow White and the Seven Dwarfs. All the posters had to have 'by kind permission of Walt Disney'.

That Christmas of 1947-48 Snow White did a short season in London and whilst there I was approached by Dixtra Enterprises asking would I like to go back to them where I would have bits to do and the salary was better; but the show was not the same, it was a mixture of No 1 and No 2 theatres and at the end of the war some of them were pretty ghastly, digs ditto (though there were some lovely landladies here and there) and the opportunity to work in Scandinavia was a big attraction. I also worked in South Africa with one of Bernard Delfont's Folies Bergere and did a few more shows for him, including the Prince of Wales Theatre in the West End. I went to Spain for George Carden the choreographer then returned at the end of my contract to do pantomime at the London Palladium (where I met my husband) followed by one last show starring Harry Secombe before I got married, stopped work, and lived abroad for the next 10 years or so. On the whole, I was very fortunate in very rarely being out of work, though in hindsight I should have been braver and not stayed with one firm for so long.

In 1977 I got a job at the National Film School for three weeks as PA to the Director whilst someone had a leave of absence. I was just a stop-gap who after a while became permanent and stayed for 15 years!

There was always a preponderance of dancers at the Theatre Girls' Club, some going on to work in revue, theatre or pantomime, others with ballet companies. Merle Park, later Royal Ballet prima ballerina, stayed there in the 1940s.[147] Also Maureen Robins, who would become a Tiller Girl, arrived at the club in the autumn months of 1946 at the age of fourteen.

Maureen Robins *(later Maureen Miles, from Sheffield, stayed at the club 1946, aged 14)*

> It is over 70 years since my visit to the Club so the memories are pretty faded. It was my first visit to London. The Club was very basic, no frills or flounces. Very sparse and cold. I recall the front door was never unlocked, one always had to ring the bell to be admitted no matter what time of day it was. If you were rehearsing late, you had to ask for a key. Luckily I never had to. My mother came to London with me for the first few days. As for me working on the stage, she was encouraging and I think a little apprehensive.
>
> Miss Bell was the person in charge (she terrified me). My impression of her was she had stepped out of an Edwardian novel. Very austere. She was probably a very nice person but to a fourteen-and-a-half year old, first time away from home, a bit scary. Sleeping arrangements were like a dormitory set out as cubicles (similar to hospital wards) with wooden side panels and curtain across the entrance, a small chest of drawers for your things. In the room I was in there were six girls. There must have been a bathroom but I can't picture it. Decor was minimal.
>
> The other thing that is fixed in my memory is breakfast: a bowl of cornflakes, help yourself to milk but one

had to present the cornflakes to Miss Bell to have the teaspoon of sugar put on them. Of course, everything was still rationed in 1946. The Second World War had only been over a year and rationing was still in full swing, things were still scarce, we still had clothing coupons so you couldn't shop 'til you dropped.

It was my first engagement with the John Tiller Girls. They recommended I stay at the Theatre Girls' Club. The Tiller School was in Old Compton Street so it was very convenient from the Theatre Girls' Club to the Tiller School; walkable and no traffic problems. If you were rehearsing, you had to be ready to work by 10 o'clock, lunch break, then rehearse in the afternoon, finish by 6 o'clock then back to the club. No money to spare for pleasure. There were two other girls from my home town, a couple of years older than me. They watched out for me and when the show started up north, one girl took me with her to her digs which I was grateful for. I worked with the Tillers for twelve years, then worked for Joan Davis for three years. Once I married I worked as a choreographer until the children arrived.

I felt safe and protected at the Theatre Girls' Club and there was kindness from colleagues. The Club has been a life saver for many, many dancers and a place where you felt secure and had the company of other dancers who passed on information about work that was available. It was reasonably priced if you were out of work or rehearsing. Personally, having two daughters who have worked in the business, I think there should be a theatre girls' club because if you have never been to London it's scary and expensive, particularly for accommodation.

Following the war, the picture is of a place of sparsity and cold, especially during the exceptionally cold months of the autumn of 1946 and the winter and spring of 1947. Another dancer staying at the club during this punishing winter was seventeen-year-old Betty Boothroyd. She came from her home town of Dewsbury to London at the invitation of the John Tiller School but quickly learned that the club and dancing were not for her. She was at the club at the time of Maureen Miles and although Maureen does not remember meeting her, she recalls one of her Tiller colleagues seeing Betty on first day of rehearsals 'but she never turned up again.' For a short time she did dance as a Tiller Girl, earning six pounds a week working in Jack Parnell's *High Time!* at the Palladium, but it was not to last. She had had romantic imaginings of theatre life and did not enjoy the reality; added to this disappointment, she riled at the Theatre Girl's Club's rules, especially when a male family friend came to visit. He managed to get into the hallway where he was greeted with open aggression by one of the club's staff, probably Agnes Bell. Betty Boothroyd is the only boarder who relates a story of a male visitor and it shows how unwelcome men were, that they were forbidden and made to know it.[148] But seventeen-year-old Betty Boothroyd did not know what Agnes Bell knew: the disappearance of Suzanne Culley, of abduction and abuse. She could not have known that the founding principle of the Theatre Girls' Club had been to provide protection to girls and young women from a society that could be extremely dangerous. Twenty-six years after her experiences at the Theatre Girls' Club, Betty Boothroyd entered politics as Labour MP for West Bromwich and she became Speaker of the House of Commons in 1992.

One who held an opposing view from Betty Boothroyd on life at the Theatre Girls' Club was thirteen-year-old Shirley Broadbent, later known as Amanda Barrie. During the austerity of the post-war years, from 1948 until 1956, the club served as a home to Amanda Barrie. In her autobiography she makes it clear how important the club and Miss Bell were to her. She was one of the youngest residents at the Theatre Girls' Club when she arrived: thirteen-years-old having just been expelled from Arts Educational at Tring. Agnes Bell would not have been unduly concerned by a child of thirteen living at the club for very young children had come there from the start. However, Amanda Barrie remembers telephone calls coming in to the club from men's organisations. There is a distinctly contradictory element to protecting girls who by the very nature of their work must go out into a world still widely regarded as hazardous, and in fulfilling her responsibilities as warden of the Theatre Girls' Club, Agnes Bell must have been balancing this contradiction for years. One telephone call (the club's number was GERRARD 1685) from a men's organisation led to a night at an American army base where, after the dancing, Amanda Barrie's companions drifted off with their chosen soldiers while she waited in the bus, eating cough sweets with one of the musicians, a Polish trombone player. [149]

Amanda Barrie's autobiography is a valuable record of what was going on inside 59 Greek Street in the late 40s. She tells of the camaraderie between the dancers at the club, the sharing of dance items and make-up, the gatherings at Leicester Square's Silver Grill to read *The Stage* and prepare for auditions in the public ladies' room at the tube station. She found work easily enough and reveals that her bed at No 59 was empty at night while she, just fourteen or fifteen years old, worked as a West End show girl. Despite Miss Bell's protective house rules, Amanda Barrie tells of night time walks through Soho to and from the Ambassadors, or the Stork Club where she worked and sometimes brushed shoulders with gangsters, of passing the Soho prostitutes who knew she was from the Theatre Girls' Club and who kept an eye out for her, of how safe she felt. For a teenager of lesser panache, this life would have been perilous. The 10 p.m. curfew may have been a necessarily flexible rule, or one that unofficially could be got round, but the question as to whether or not Miss Bell knew of the very young Amanda Barrie's all-night work routine is a moot one.[150]

Two performers already at the club when Amanda Barrie arrived there found their way into the pages of the *Kensington Post* when, in their case despairing of stage work, they started-up a dress-agency. Lilian and Marie (the paper did not think it necessary to give surnames) met at the Theatre Girls' Club in the autumn of 1947, Lilian was just de-mobbed from E.N.S.A., Marie straight from the Oldham Repertory Company hoping to get work in a West End theatre. Sales items were donated by actor friends and displayed in their Westbourne Grove shop window. Over Easter 1948, dresses, handbags and shoes were displayed emerging from a 'large Easter egg split open' with a notice saying "hatched on no coupons".[151] The moment stage work came in, they closed-up shop.

Mary Wylie *(from Edinburgh, stayed at the club in 1948, aged 17)*

> I had thought of going to Edinburgh University to study medicine, I wanted to be a psychiatrist, then I got a grant of £100 for a whole year from the Edinburgh Council to study at the Old Vic School of Drama in London. It was [someone] at the Old Vic who suggested I stay at the Theatre Girls' Club. The warden Miss Bell had lovely white hair and a dog called Brandy. She had a lot of power and liked to make people cry.

She made me cry. There were about sixteen girls at the club when I was there, and three staff who were not treated very nicely.   Mrs Lough [?] a Scottish/Indian who had been promised the wardenship of the club, the cook Miss Finney who was Irish, and Jackie, a dancer, second-in-command to Miss Bell.

We boarders thought Miss Bell owned the club. It was safe but it was also cold and miserable. No heating, not much to eat. One piece of toast at breakfast, but we were on war-time rations then. I remember Miss Finney sometime bought eggs; I think it was from her own pocket. We used to wash our own dishes. There was one bathroom which was opened on request and we did our laundry in a room up at the top of the building. There was a flat iron and a gas ring on a meter. I never told my mother how bad it was. But Soho was very neighbourly. The shop keepers knew you.

My friend Margaret Wilson and I were very straight-laced. Margaret was a singer at the Royal College of Music and used the piano in the cellar for her practice. Fay Compton would come to the club for lunch, and Compton Mackenzie.

Apart from a spell with Glasgow's Citizens' Theatre Company, Mary Wylie remained in London after her training at the Old Vic. She took a part in the television show *Emergency Ward Ten* but within a few years had, according to her friend Margaret Wilson, 'given up thoughts of acting as it was very difficult trying to get into London productions and she would not consider touring or working out of London.'

Margaret Dobson *(later Wilson) (from Durham, stayed at the club in 1948, aged 18)*

I seem to remember that Mary [Wylie] arrived at the TGC just a little later than I did. We both hated London at first as it seemed so overpowering. However, we soon found Hyde and St James' parks and the Embankment and much of our weekend time was spent walking through and along them. I was from a working-class family where there was no money to spare for anything but the bare essentials, but love and care were in abundance. I had two older brothers. My father had a sweet true tenor voice which must have given me a love of music from birth as he sang lullabies to me. My mother played piano. My first performance was at the age of 3 years singing 'Jesus loves me' in a chapel anniversary celebration. I won a scholarship to the one grammar school in the area [then] my grandparents paid for me to have singing lessons from a coal-miner, Mr. George Griffiths, who was conductor of a popular mail voice choir. When he advised me to study with someone beyond his limits I eventually began to have weekly lessons with Molly de Gunst, an Australian soprano who had sung with Sadlers Wells Opera Co before marrying.

This was the beginning of my music education in earnest... My intentions were to get to university for an English degree with which to teach. However, my current music teacher, together with the County Music Adviser insisted that I should apply to the Royal College of Music. This I did without expecting to be accepted but I was. I was given a discretionary grant to study singing and piano there for 3 years. I believe it was £140 per year, out of which I paid £60 to the Royal College of Music.

Having scoured all possible sources, I despaired of finding accommodation that would enable me to take up my place until finding, in the Theatre Girls' Club small print, that students would be considered if vacancies were available. Even YWCA and Salvation Army hostels were not as cheap as the thirty shillings per week of the TGC!! My only other visit to London had been for the entrance exams. I'd never been away from home before, not even for a holiday. When I arrived (it was a grey September morning when my Dad with tears in his eyes put me on the train leaving Durham for London) I lugged my suitcase to find Foyle's Bookshop in Charing Cross Road, having been informed that there was an alleyway through the building that would lead me straight into Greek St., in fact virtually opposite No. 59. With an enormous sense of relief, I shot across the road and rang the bell. Eventually, I heard a chain being pulled on the door prior to its meagre opening, and a thin, angular, anxious, suspicious face (she later turned out to be Jackie) appeared to ask what I wanted. On telling her that I was a student with booked accommodation, she rejected this, saying that students were not allowed there and that the warden, Miss Bell, had not informed her of any expected new arrival. She then said she would have to check with Miss Bell, shut and locked the door again and left me, absolutely panic-stricken on the doorstep!! After some time, the door was re-opened by a small, slight figure of stern demeanour, pale-complexioned and bespectacled, with white hair taken back in rigid waves to a bun, and dressed in dark clothing. This was Miss Bell.

Miss Bell seemed pretty old but then we were very young. On reflection, the air of control that she exuded could have been due to circumstance beyond our ken. Perhaps insecurity about the fact that she was an ageing single lady who would not be able to keep that job in perpetuum. Life was very different in those day for any such person unless they had a good, solid private income for their old age. Also, having to cope with and cater for such a constantly-changing and widely-varied group of residents in times of rationing together with very modest payments coming in would have required a certain degree of strict supervision.

After my stressful admission to the TGC, I was shown to my 'room' which turned out to be one of the 'horse-boxes' positioned along the passageway that ran parallel to the large lounge. Each one was furnished with a small chest of drawers, a single bed, a small wooden upright chair, hooks (?) for clothes and a curtain for the entrance. [Later] I moved to the top floor which housed the large laundry room (with door onto the roof) and, across the passage, a multi-bedded room in which Mary slept, plus an inner box room into which I was placed. Miss Bell would suddenly ask us why we hadn't found other accommodation as the TGC was not for students!! Then would follow a frantic couple of weeks or so desperately scanning newspapers to see if we could find anything affordable... in vain. On braving a trip to Miss Bell's office (holy of holies!) on the first floor to impart this news, we'd be told not to be silly, that of course we could stay longer. So there was the odd flash of humanity. Miss Bell treated me very differently later.

At the end of my first contract, a 6-month tour with Emile Littler's production of 'Lilac Time'. I had to have my badly-infected tonsils removed in Newcastle. After six months, I set off again, on an overnight bus to London, arriving just in time for the opening of the 'out of work theatricals' labour exchange from which I was sent for interview for a clerical post in the Calor Gas headquarters in Oxford Street, then straight to the TGC where I reported in before making myself an instant coffee in the laundry room. I was amazed to be given a single room on the second floor.

From then on, I found Miss Bell to be far more human, more solicitous about my well-being and even lending me a simple sewing-machine so that I could make myself a skirt. I don't remember ever venturing further along the passage where the Chapel was situated. This sounds crazy but I suppose I always felt on probation and therefore would feel that certain areas were out of bounds, but the craziest reason was, I had heard the story about the ghost that haunted that floor being that of Virginia Compton who had died in her room there. Her 'walkings' were always associated with a sudden aroma of lavender filling the air. Guess who occasionally was conscious of a gentle wafting of lavender in her room for no apparent reason!

It was very cold in winter. Mary was quite lucky in being heavily time-tabled on her course at the Old Vic, so escaped the cold after breakfast until her return in the evening. My college time-table meant that I spent the major part of the day in the club, practicing singing and piano in the basement, then filling hot-water-bottle and donning dressing-gown and scarf over clothes to write essays and work on Harmony & Counterpoint, etc. in bed! We could never pop across the road for coffee as we were living on a shoe-string, so had nothing left with which to even visit the college canteen for bread roll & cheese when missing lunch at the club. My Dad would send tins of Ambrosia milk.... so Mary and I would boil the kettle in the Laundry and make up two mugs of Ambrosia, relishing the first half as a drink before stuffing in as many cornflakes (acquired via putting together any pennies that could be spared) as possible. Mmm... what comfort! The bathroom was kept locked most of the time. One was very lucky if able to catch it open for a weekly bath. Mary and I performed most of our ablutions in the huge white pot sinks in the laundry room with its bare concrete floor, often with cold winds whistling through the door to the roof.

I'm ashamed to say that I knew nothing about Jackie, except an impression that she had been a dancer. She was somehow just vaguely there on the periphery... small, slight, terrier-like, pale and constantly-anxious face, greying-brown hair pulled tightly back except for curled fringe, always darting in and out. She was Miss Bell's 2nd in command but seemed very subservient to her. Nessie Tierney was probably in her late fifties, quite tall, long grey wavy hair plus a curly fringe. I was given to understand that she worked for Equity, possibly as a rep, so she was a great source of advice to many actresses, dancers, singers etc. It appeared that the TGC had become her permanent residence in which she seemed quite comfortable and at ease. Apparently, she had been a dancer when younger.

I found a really good teacher, Bruce Boyce, a Canadian baritone.[152] He and his wife were so kind to me as I could only go straight from work, so they would provide me with fruit juice or coffee on my arrival. I had only a few months before my Dad telephoned me the news that a telegram had arrived for me from D'Oyly Carte Opera offering me a contract... and as a result I began touring with DOC for almost 5 years before returning North to be with my mother who was in a state of collapse after my lovely, caring Dad died of a heart-attack at the age of just 56 years. It took approximately two years for my mother to be able to start getting on with life, by which time a meaningful relationship was beginning to get under way... leading to marriage, three children etc! I was never back in the TGC again.

Margaret Wilson also remembers visits to the Theatre Girls' Club by an eight-year-old Alan Howard who had stolen the show at his great-grandmother Virginia Compton's eighty-six birthday party in 1940. The extended Compton family remained closely connected to the Theatre Girls' Club; family members visited from time to time and Compton Mackenzie filled the role of club president until a year before its closure.

Sheila Rennie *(from Brechin in Scotland, stayed at the club in 1949, aged 19)*

I went to Arts Educational, Lees Place, Mayfair, which at that time was a small establishment known as the Cone Ripman School: after three Cone sisters and a Miss Ripman. Leslie Crowther was there then. I stayed for five terms. I moved to the Theatre Girls' Club in 1949 when I was nineteen years old and had a friend there called Catherine May. It was mainly dancers at the club. The bedrooms were like hospital wards and Miss Bell was okay. I got my first job through *The Stage,* and had stints at Watford and Swindon repertories, also Paignton and Luton.

In 1950 I left the Theatre Girls' Club for the Interval Club on Dean Street. At nights we slept at No. 1 Soho Square. The Interval Club was a mixed club so I preferred it to the Theatre Girls' Club. I met my husband, Philip James there and after we married, in 1953, I gave up work because Philip wanted to keep family and working life separate. When he died, I started working again on *Keeping Up Appearances* from 1985. My last job was in 1995.

And so, the club in the 1940s was cold and, during the five years of the war, cold and dark. There were drama and music students staying there, although the majority seems always to have been dancers all woefully underpaid, and the dance students could be as young as thirteen. Miss Bell, who accepted these children and young women through the club's doors, is remembered variously. Her hair turned white, and with Brandy the dog for company, some of the boarders found her too severe, others helpful. There was also an early rumour, which persisted for some years, of Virginia Compton's ghost roaming the second floor, leaving behind her a fragrance of lavender.

PART IV
The 1950s

8
The Beginning of Change

Hundreds of girls and young women hoping for work of all kinds came to London each year wholly unprepared for life there. By the 1950s the few policewomen attached to the Metropolitan Police had been given the task of seeking these visitors out.

> Every night or two, as many as five or six of these young creatures might be stopped ...and questioned about themselves. They were invariably homeless, mostly from the provinces or country, attracted to London by a genuine desire to work. Without the necessary qualifications, and with no idea of where to find employment, they drifted about the streets, sleeping in parks and open spaces, ready prey indeed for those ready to pounce on such unwary victims.[153]

The London Council for the Welfare of Women and Girls, an affiliation of public authority and voluntary bodies which appears to have functioned under the auspices of the London Diocesan Council, published in 1950 a warning to those parents who let their young daughters come to London unprepared.

> Office girls earn small wages: housing them is often a matter of cost. Some hostels will take 16-year-olds if they can pay the fees – usually 35s a week and up. But wardens are very

reluctant to take younger girls. Fifteen-year-olds who get jobs in small factories or workrooms are the most difficult group of all. They usually work in London's outer fringe. Social workers are greatly concerned about them...Ballet pupils are the youngest and need special hostels because of their hours of work. A place like the Theatre Girls' Club is invaluable but its space is limited.[154]

This describes a world barely changed from that of Maude Stanley's time. Girls and young women were coming to London to face the same dangers as those of the late-Victorian years, but some children training for theatrical performance away from home had a safe place to stay thanks to the Theatre Girls' Club. The Interval Club, two streets away at 22 Dean Street, was providing much the same service. Founded in 1926 by Mary Balvaird Hewett of the Catholic Stage Guild, the Interval Club offered accommodation to theatre workers but with one notable difference from its close neighbour the Theatre Girls' Club – it was open to young men as well as women, made possible through separate sleeping quarters for women at 1 Soho Square. Its atmosphere was more relaxed than the Theatre Girls' Club. Even so, Rosemary Carter, a stage manager who stayed at the Interval Club in 1953, said it was run by 'an elderly lady who was very protective.'[155] This would be Miss Molly Hewett, Mary Hewett's daughter, described by another as 'a strong character' who reportedly called the Queen's mother 'ducky' over the phone.[156]

The Interval Club held its twenty-seventh anniversary luncheon party on Sunday, 1st March 1953. Actor Patricia Hayes, also a member of the Catholic Stage Guild, was there, and Compton Mackenzie who gave a speech which he started with: 'I have come as a kind of emissary from the neighbouring High Anglican club founded by my mother – the Theatre Girls' Club, bringing greetings.'[157]   In Virginia Compton's time the impression is distinctly of a club religious in character, but less so after her death in 1940. Arthur Winnington-Ingram and Father Kingdon were no longer there to pay their pastoral visits which Virginia Compton had always felt to be 'occasions of very special thanksgiving.'[158]   The Bishop of St Albans, Michael Furse, filled the place left empty by the death of the Bishop of London in 1939 until his resignation in 1944, but what happened thereafter is difficult to say. Although the chapel on the second floor was remembered, there is no mention within living memory, from the mid-1940s onwards, of boarders going to services or of confirmations taking place there. 'I don't remember any religious atmosphere,' says Audrey Crockett who stayed at the club in 1944.[159]   By this time the daily running of the club was firmly in the hands of the club's supervisor, Agnes Bell.

If Agnes Bell was raised in the Presbyterian tradition, which as a Scot she probably was, then the atmosphere in the club under her control would be very different from the days of Virginia Compton. Miss Bell impressed herself strongly on the minds of those who met and remember her: wavy white hair tied in a bun, the large bunch of keys hanging from a belt at her waist, the little dog nicknamed Bandy Bell at her heels; yet her character is elusive. Some newcomers to the club felt that she judged them harshly, that she rewarded those she liked and came down hard on those she did not, which somewhat fits the mould of the Presbyterian mind. 'She was a cool, cold character, remote,' recalls Margaret Dobson who stayed at the club in the 1940s when Miss Bell would have been in her sixties, 'but I sometimes wonder if it wasn't shyness.'[160]   And so, Miss Bell must remain something of an enigma; but it can be adduced from the memories of those who lived under her rule at the Theatre Girls' Club that she was inclined to show favouritism, although this is recalled only by those who were not favoured.

By the 1950s Agnes Bell had been in sole control of the daily running of the club for ten years. Some boarders thought she was its owner. In that time, there seems to have been no relaxing of the rules and regulations which had so upset Betty Boothroyd and Mary Wylie. Yet, Amanda Barrie was one who got on well with Agnes Bell. The club's restrictions did not seem to curtail her activities during her regular stays at the club between 1948 and 1956 when she worked in nightclubs as a teenager, but when she started working regularly for day-time television as well as at Winston's on Clifford Street at night, the club (presumably Miss Bell) would not let her stay longer.[161]

As to Soho in the 1950s, Greek Street's House of Charity was still running a few doors up and across from the club, also the Budapest public house and restaurant, where the post office had been in Maude Stanley's time. The Pillars of Hercules, meeting place of journalists, continued a little farther down at the entrance to Manette Street (from where Margaret Dobson had emerged in 1948 into Greek Street straight off the train from Durham) as did the restaurant L'Escargot nine doors down from the club. The tight-knit Soho community was intact. Soho 'was very neighbourly,' Mary Wylie said 'the shopkeepers knew you.'[162]

Its streets had 'bakeries, patisseries, delicatessens,.... pimps, pansies and prostitutes less handsome than the fashionable demi-mondaines of Soho's long ago,

'...agents, publishers, song-pluggers, crooners and band
leaders talking about picking up royalties for broadcasts on

air. There are barrow boys with wads of cabbage and the Greyhound Express, movie men from Wardour Street with loud ties and cigars, small time prize fighters with their managers, racecourse touts, waiters, beggars, drinking clubs, rehearsal rooms and sound of Le Jazz Hot, bookshops with thinly veneered pornography...[163]

That the girls and young women living at the Theatre Girls' Club were able, safely and confidently, to go about Soho's streets even in the dead of night, says volumes about the people in its area. The district belonged to its restaurateurs, public house licensees, club owners and the remaining trades and crafts of the likes of bakers, tailors and musical instrument makers; the criminals seemed to take on the character of burrowing predators and to keep the violence within their own ranks.

Soho's traders and restaurateurs held their first street fair in July 1955 by way of showing to the outside world that Soho's square mile was not all bullying gangsters, sex shops and crime. It was claimed that more people turned out in Soho than to that year's Lord Mayor's Show.[164] There is no mention in newspaper reports of the Theatre Girls' Club taking part in these festivities which passed outside its doors but doubtless the residents were out in the sunshine watching the waiters' race and the spaghetti-eaten-with-chop-sticks competition.

The visibility of soliciting women which had been complained about by the more respectable residents during the early 1900s was still a vexation to the authorities. Women prostitutes 'stood in the doorways twirling their bunches of keys,' said one young woman staying at the Interval Club in the early 1950s.[165] Between 1954 and 1957 Yorkshireman John Wolfenden chaired a parliamentary committee to look into laws covering homosexuality and prostitution. Homosexual relations between men had been punished for a very long time under laws made for men by men; no law applied to women despite an attempt at it in 1921 which did not pass through the Lords. The Wolfenden committee recommended that anyone over the age of twenty-one should not be prosecuted for a sexual act taking place in private and with consent. It did, though, '[set] its face against any form of licencing prostitutes or brothels.'[166] Its response to open solicitation was to recommend a clean-up of London's streets through the expedient of higher penalties for soliciting. The prostitutes of Greek Street retreated indoors and then, in 1959, the Street Offences Act sealed it: 'It shall be an offence for a person 18 or over (whether male or female) persistently to loiter or solicit in a street or public place for the purpose of prostitution.'[167] There was no penalty for the buyer.

The 1950s was the decade in which Soho's streets became less obviously a place where the sexual services of woman or man could be bought. Now invitations to the transaction were pinned on the doors of Soho's ancient buildings: 'model looking for work, apply within'; or negotiated discretely within the clubs. Amanda Barrie says the only time she had any trouble in Soho was now, when the sex workers were forced off the streets. A punter, unable to find what he was after, found his way into the Theatre Girls' Club and to her bedside. Luckily, a patrolling policeman saw the break-in and took the intruder away.[168] Even Miss Bell could not unfailingly stop the dangerous and unsavoury from finding a way into the club. For all the years she was there she must have been constantly aware of the possibility while knowing it was impossible to perfectly secure the building. There was access to the building from Bateman's Buildings at the back. Residents would sometimes go out onto a flat roof outside the laundry windows to sunbathe and the more daring would make night time escapes into Soho via this route.

In the 1950s Soho's pimps and gangsters were flourishing. By now two men, Billy Hill and Bert Marsh, were regarded as England's leading Mafiosi. Bert Marsh's minder, Albert Dimes, was a gangster who frequented Winston's during Amanda Barrie's time there. In the summer of 1955, the year of the first Soho fair, Albert Dimes had a running knife battle through the streets of Soho with his rival, Jack Spot. Street attacks in broad daylight occurred with alarming frequency within so small a community, and police raids of clubs and drug dens were regularly witnessed. In 1958 Paul Raymond opened his Revue Bar in Walker's Court. Here was a strip club of unparalleled excesses, 'the biggest and smartest strip club in London' offering animated nudity and sex enactments.[169] This world of prurient entertainment was but a short step away, literal and metaphorical, from the lives of the residents at the Theatre Girls' Club. Compton Mackenzie associated with Paul Raymond and, by extension, George Harrison Marks, pornographic film-maker and photographer whose studio was in Gerrard Street, just down from Greek Street. It was Harrison Marks who took the publicity photographs for Bernard Delfont's inaugural Folies Bergere show in 1952, in which some of the dancers at the Theatre Girls' Club worked.[170]

It was a cocktail of attitudes and life-styles which characterised life at the Theatre Girls' Club in the 1950s with its austere and protective supervisor Miss Bell, its urbane and open-minded president Edward Compton Mackenzie and its ambitious young boarders rubbing shoulders with theatre impresarios, nightclub owners and the occasional gangster. Since its opening in 1915, boarders from all spectrums of the social order had come there: girls knocking on the front door asking for shelter and youngsters from working- and middle-class families forging their futures with varying degrees of

91

confidence and success. Each responded in different ways to life in London but one constant is a collective feeling that they were safe within the club and on the streets of Soho. Agnes Bell was guarding against the likes of Suzanne Culley's John who offered motor rides to trusting girls then made them disappear.

Helen Bignell *(later Helen Locke) (from Smethwick, stayed 1954, aged 15)*

> I first stayed at the Theatre Girls' Club 1954-55 and on and off until 1963. I was living at home before that. My parents liked it as it was a place to safely stay in London while auditioning or rehearsing. It was central and *safe*. I heard of it from dancers and variety artistes in my first show. Miss Bell, who greeted me, seemed quite strict but very helpful. I stayed for short periods on numerous occasions, sometimes in a 6/8 bed dormitory type room with curtains around the beds. I wasn't shocked by Greek Street. At first I was too naïve to understand what these ladies were doing on the street. I found them kind as they would often walk me back to the club – but perhaps they were just protecting their business interests. I only went to London when auditioning or rehearsing and made no especial friends, but I felt safe and didn't find the club's curfew oppressive. If you had tickets for a show Miss Bell would let you stay out later. Later on I continued in tours, summer seasons and pantomime until I married in October 1963, then I worked in shops as a demonstrator then a finance company until 1969 when I had a family. It would be very helpful for young women to have a safe haven in London. I never enjoyed being in London but

felt safe at the club. I introduced at least half-a-dozen girls who I met in various shows to it (they hadn't heard of it).

In the summer of 1957 Shirley Jones from Stratford-on-Avon arrived at the club. She had studied domestic science before coming to London to work as a nanny. How she progressed from nanny to aspiring actor staying at the Theatre Girls' Club is a mystery but she got a job playing Little Red Riding Hood at Lowestoft's Arcadia Theatre's pantomime that year.[171]   Another resident was Hannah Gordon, later known for her role in the 1970s show *Upstairs Downstairs* and for her film and theatre performances.

Blue Bell Girl, actor and novelist Helene Thornton, variously known as Elaine Smith and Hellen Torren, stayed at the club in the late 1950s. She appeared in The Edgar Wallace Mysteries and The Liquidator before marrying Jess Yates of *Stars on Sunday*. Her daughter Paula Yates in turn married Bob Geldorf. Actor Lois Daine, who came to London for the first time in 1957, befriended Helene Thornton, whom she knew as 'Elaine Smith from Blackpool' when they lived together at the Theatre Girls' Club.

Lois Daine *(family name Dainty, from Blackpool, age 16, 1957)*

> I always wanted to be an actress. I worked as a dancer when I was sixteen at Blackpool – *Sunday Night at Blackpool* the show was called, I think it was televised from the Palace or the Opera House – and I managed to save £100 which took me to London. I was so excited. I think it was Stella Tanner of the Tanner Sisters who told me about the Theatre Girls' Club, but anyway, that's where I stayed.
>
> I got a train and travelled down to London all alone, pure as the driven snow. I was very ambitious. I didn't have a job to go to but I was going to be a star before the end of

93

the year! At the Theatre Girls' Club there was a bell which rang for breakfast and I would go down in my pyjamas with something or other over the top because it was quite cold. The inside of the Theatre Girls' Club was plain, nothing special, but it was my first *entre* into London. I was so glad to be with actresses and away from dancers. The dancers were a tough lot. In Blackpool they called me "cry baby". I became friendly with Helene Thornton. She was a bit older than me. There were chaps at the door and all of that. She was kind.

I slept in a dormitory and remember looking out of the window onto Greek Street. I didn't know anything much about Soho and used to wander around. I really enjoyed the Italian restaurant nearby and ate spaghetti there for the first time, and I'd visit agents every day. You could use any number of agents then and I did walk-ons and crowd scenes – you know, a view of the back of my head. There was the agent Eric Blythe whose office was in Leicester Square I think. And I had a boyfriend who was into existentialism, Satre. I soaked it up as you do, like a sponge. Then I went back to Blackpool to play in George and Alfred Black's *Friends and Neighbours* at the Grand Theatre. It's a beautiful theatre.

I came back to London when *Friends and Neighbours* transferred to the Victoria Palace but I didn't go back to the Theatre Girls' Club. I stayed in a flat in Earls Court and signed with the agent Beryl Seaton. Every time I had an audition I would go in to see her and she would put a bow in my hair and make sure I had enough lipstick and powder. Even then I felt she was old-fashioned. When London Management wanted to sign me I had to pay Beryl to release me from my contract. Anyhow, Clive Goodwin at Granada cast me in *Ticket for Tomorrow* with Richard Briers and, well, it just went on from there. I only ever went back to Blackpool to visit my parents.

Lois Daine married actor Tom Bell and since 2010 has written three plays encouraged by the Actors' Centre in the Severn Dials, London. Two have been staged.

Anna Sharkey *(stayed late-1950s, age 17)*

When I first hit London, poor and starving, I lived in a place called the Theatre Girls' Club, for £2 a week. It was run by a very strict Presbyterian lady who was more strict than the nuns at the convent I had just left. One could only have a bath if one was rehearsing so if you were a student, like me – I studied classical dancing and singing – you just had to queue up. We used to go to the swimming baths or exchange our pudding for somebody's late night [bathroom] key. This was all in the middle of Soho with prostitutes all over the streets. There we were – this house being run like a convent.

We were really very innocent then at seventeen. The big "Sexy-Sixties" didn't hit us until the seventies. It was a lovely happy time and there was never any feeling of danger. Maybe the people with money were leading [the] drugs and rock 'n' roll lifestyle, we were just children living and working in the theatre.[172]

PART V
1960-1971

9
Change

The Tropicana Club, advertised as an All Girl Strip Revue, opened at 18 Greek Street in competition with Raymond's Revue Bar in May 1959. When it closed two years later it was 'the seediest of beer sodden atmospheres... the windows were swagged in oceans of red velvet curtains... there were discarded G-strings, used condoms, plastic chandeliers – all the tawdry remains of a former strip club.'[173] So said Wendy Cook when Peter Cook and Nicholas Luard took the building over in 1961 as the Establishment Club, offering satirical humour to a private membership. Another Soho club just opened was Ronnie Scott's on Gerrard Street, offering the world's greatest jazz. And 60 Greek Street, which as the Austro-Hungarian Club had created such disturbance to the occupiers of Maude Stanley's Soho Club & Home for Working Girls in the 1890s, was now home to the 1960s Le Kilt Club. The regime that had characterised life at the Theatre Girls' Club at 59 Greek Street for over forty years, the locked doors, the Victorian décor, scant bathroom provision, all were in their last days. The 1960s, like the 1920s, was a decade of social change.

Of the many dancers staying at the club in the early '60s, one came from Ireland, another from Birmingham. Both sixteen-years-old.

Audrey Corr *(from Sandy Cove, Dun Laoghaire, Ireland, 1960, aged 16)*

> [I] and another Irish innocent went over to stay at the Theatre
> Girls' Club in London. We were the only two dancers there

who weren't strippers at the Windmill. [I] wouldn't have dreamed of letting any of [my] own children make such a journey at such a young age, but incredible innocence is protection in a way. We hadn't got a clue. [The other girls] couldn't believe that the two of us had reached the age we had without losing our virginity. They were fascinated by us and they looked after us... we were a novelty to them. They never said that they were protecting us, you'd just turn around and find them beside you. Particularly when we left London and began to tour. Many of the girls were in their thirties and to be in the Theatre Girls' Club at that age meant that their futures could be pretty grim.[174]

Jane Terry *(from Birmingham, stayed 1961-1962, aged 16)*

I stayed at the Theatre Girls' Club as a dancer in 1961/62 rehearsing for summer season. I think the lady who ran it was called Miss Bell? I'd been doing panto, Sinbad the Sailor, at the Alexandra Theatre in Birmingham and I asked one of the girls how I could get summer season and she told me to look in *The Stage* and that I could stay in London at the Theatre Girls' Club. I came down to audition for a Bernard Delfont summer season and got the job so I stayed at the club while we rehearsed at the Max River studios. The food was very basic and you were given a sandwich for your lunch on your rehearsal days! I remember I lost weight the week of rehearsing. Then we went to Weymouth to the Alexandra Gardens for the season.

It was fun staying at the Theatre Girls' Club. I can remember us girls used to throw pennies from the bedroom windows at the ladies of the night in Greek Street. I stayed in the front room. The beds had curtains. Oh, another thing was a picture of Christ in the chapel at the club. The girls used to say his eyes followed you wherever you were in the room, or winked at you!!! I could never see it happening and the girls used to say 'Jane, you're standing in the wrong place'. We were very young. I think the chapel was on the second floor.

Four or five of us would go down into the basement after dinner to rehearse. There was a piano down there but we didn't use it. I stayed at the club in 1962 during rehearsals for the Butlins summer season in Filey. There was a girl at the club called Sally (I'm almost sure her name was Sally Hansell) who was going out with Jimmy Clitheroe. She used to do my hair for me but she died in a car crash later.

This was twenty years on from the days of Virginia Compton. Her chapel remained and a fine portrait of her hung on the club room wall but memory of her was fading while the story of her ghost was vividly remembered by Marilyn Rogers.

Marilyn Rogers *(later McConnell) (from Nottingham, 1962, aged 18)*

I stayed at the Theatre Girls' Club in 1962/3. I'd been an art student but it wasn't financially possible when I reached 18 and had to pay. I got a job as a teaching assistant at a private school, teaching art and music and movement, but it didn't start until after Christmas so I saw an ad for dancers for Agencia Productions' panto in Kidderminster, I auditioned in Skegness, got in and went off. I loved it!! Everyone was wishing me well in my new teaching job and – I didn't want to go! I knew where I belonged. The girls in panto had told me to look in *The Stage* for the ads. I saw an ad for dancers at Rhyl and rang the Risco Agency about auditions. They asked me to send a photo, measurements and details, which I did. After a few days I got a contract through the post. That's when I went to London, green as grass, and booked in at the YWCA. Then I joined another girl who I got speaking to at rehearsals in other digs (with an exploding boiler) for one night only. We asked others who were at rehearsals where they were staying and they told us about the Theatre Girls' Club. We thought it sounded nice. Others in the show were staying there and we wanted to feel part of the company (and not blown up!). When I arrived at the club it was dark, lots of dark panelling everywhere and slippery flooring. An elderly lady showed us to our beds and gave us a brief chat about rules. My friend vanished with her to another dorm. I felt a bit lost and didn't know what to do next.

Up in the dormitories the single iron beds were divided by heavy linen curtains – like old fashioned hospitals, and there was a small bedside cabinet for each girl. I can't remember the loos or showers. After choosing a book from the bookcase and chatting to one of the girls who was a regular and told me about the ghost and the chapel, I said goodnight and tried to snuggle down, feeling very uneasy and a bit disappointed that the lights went out before I could read the book. That's when I got really scared of the ghost and started to cry quietly as I could into the pillow. The girl next door heard me, she was so sweet – oh you poor thing! she said and pulled my mattress on the floor next to her bed. (Wasn't that kind). It didn't help when I saw the picture in the hall of Virginia Compton holding the same book (or so I though) as I had chosen.

There were strict rules – no male visitors, no coming down to breakfast in dressing gown or with hair in rollers. After breakfast we queued up at the sink with our plate and took turns with the dish mop under the cold running water. You know, I can remember one favoured young lady, very pretty with big brown eyes, sitting at the huge round table at breakfast in a pink housecoat and rollers in her hair right next to Miss whatever-her-name [who] frightened the living daylights out of me! No reason just how I felt. But it was definitely safer than any grotty B&B we could afford, and apart from the ghost which put the wind up me, I had no negative experiences and I didn't find the curfew oppressive and Greek Street didn't shock me really – I liked it honestly! We just got on with where we were going.

We would set off to Max Rivers rehearsal rooms after breakfast. We were rehearsing for summer season at Rhyl Pavilion and another group were rehearsing for another summer show. I was in awe of the girls looking so glamourous. I quickly learned how to hitch up the legs of my leotard, tie my shirt under my bust and to wear plimsoles or heels, not ballet flats! It was before the miniskirts, and dancers wore their hair up. Some of the Tiller Girls were there at the club, and one girl was in agony because she had to rehearse in character shoes and fishnet tights. Fishnet tights in those days were not the soft light nylon ones worn today – they were coarse heavy elastic with a hefty seam from top to bottom. The seam had rubbed a huge raw blister down the back of her ankle and the hard leather shoes had left a bloody sore which, despite plasters and cotton wool, was getting worse and worse. Poor girl went hobbling off to rehearsals but seemed to think she would not be allowed to leave off the tights or shoes.

Auditioning was a good way to get a free class with a top-class teacher. We would often go along even when we didn't fit the criteria at all. The Theatre Girls' Club was right in the middle of town and so convenient. Sometimes there were droves of us going down the road from one audition to the other. There were often 12 girls and boys in a production, so there was always something somewhere. We'd all crowd the notice board at Max Rivers, or wait for the first *Stage* to appear on Thursday at Leicester Square. We were encouraged to join Equity... but in the end we just rolled up to as many auditions as we could, and if we got the job we were always offered an Equity contract. Working abroad was a very dodgy proposition. The white slave trade was rife we were told. Also you had to toughen up – no egg shell feelings because the dancers got the blame for almost everything. Or so it seemed.

I did various pantos and summer seasons. My friend Jayne and I were at Clacton Pier when a reporter from the *Daily Mail* came to interview everyone. Jayne and I didn't want to do this, so we nipped off to get something to eat. Half way to the restaurant we heard the reporter call us "Hi girls! Mind if I join you?" Being polite, we took her to the café. This smarty-pants reporter had her notepad under the table and noted *everything* we said! Mugs!! This was Lynda Lee Porter!! The article appeared in the national papers and the company we were with hauled us up and gave us a lecture on loyalty. Not our finest hour but we got panto out of it with the choreographer!

After my time at the Theatre Girls Club and during auditions, my Australian friend Cherie from my first summer show worked at the Plaza Cinema in Piccadilly and I stayed with her and got a job at the Plaza too. That was a beautiful cinema with a wardrobe dept for our green tailored usherette suits. The bosses liked dancers for their ability to stand nicely and we were allowed to go off for auditions or go back after having been off in panto or whatever. Another great friend was Jayne. We shared many a grotty bedsit. The first time I worked abroad was with Jayne. It was cabaret in Oslo. It was great fun... and after a summer season at Butlins Clacton I was asked if I'd like to tour Italy... so off I went. We toured over 70 theatres in 6 months by coach. It was a wonderful way to see the real Italy.

I met my husband Bob, stage manager at the Ice Drome in Blackpool in 1972. I was there each summer until '74, then came a brief episode where I skated in Germany but left there to join a German dance troupe. I worked with George Anthony Night Stars for about a year then went back to England to get married. I opened a dancing school, made costumes for a local firm, had 3 children and retired at 60. I still dance and do fitness stuff and treasure the lovely friends I met on the way. Girls today probably wouldn't think a place like the Theatre Girls' Club is needed but I bet a lot of parents would be relieved! Girls wouldn't tolerate being told what to do like that these days, I'm sure.

By the early 1960s, Agnes Bell, who had frightened the living daylights out of the eighteen-year-old Marilyn Rogers and brought Mary Wylie to tears, now was approaching her eightieth birthday. She had maintained a tight ship at the Theatre Girls' Club for forty years but the rules and restrictions of the 1920s could not carry on into the 1960s although, astonishingly, they did for as long as Miss Bell was its guiding spirit. The Beatles, The Rolling Stones, Carnaby Street, Biba, Twiggy, James Bond captured the nation's imagination, while within the walls of 59 Greek Street, the dark panelling and slippery flooring recalled by Marilyn Rogers, the keys and locks, the suspicions about visiting male friends experienced by Betty Boothroyd continued in a parallel reality.

The 1960s and 1970s are supposed to have been years of female liberation, a time when the attitudes dominant in the days of Maude Stanley were left behind, but these two decades can only boast of having been the slender dawn of a gender equality which is still being negotiated in the 2020s. In the 1960s, predatory behaviour towards women was still 'almost accepted' says journalist Joan Bakewell, 'there was no route for doing anything about it.'[175] That said, the 1960s did see some changes in behaviour and attitude which benefited women. It began to be acknowledged that the majority possessed no autonomy because of their financial dependence upon the men in their lives. The Married Women's Property Act of 1882 had allowed a wife to retain control over her private income but this was of no help to those with no income at all. For most middle class and certainly working class women with no private income, the Married Women's Property Act was meaningless. A revision passed in 1964 gave a married woman a legal right to keep half of any savings she might make from money given to her by her husband as house-keeping, but this amounted to next to nothing and was of no help to those needing to escape violent or bullying partners. Refuges for women and their children began to appear. Then poorly paid women car workers, clothing workers, night cleaners, began industrial action in protest against this institutionally entrenched financial disability.

Slowly, more legislation eased the lives of women. Until the Abortion Act of 1967 which legalised abortion on certain grounds, termination of pregnancy was against British law. The Act of 1967 is profoundly telling for it opens an unflinching eye on the lives of countless previous generations of women delivering babies in secret, babies sometimes abandoned, 'bastard' children, countless babies taken for adoption, and medically treacherous back-street abortions. Generations of fear, trauma and shame brought down upon the heads of women by those who do not carry the unborn but who are programmed to seek the sexual pleasure that produces them.[176]

It was from these horrors that the Maude Stanleys and the Virginia Comptons of their day wanted to save young women by bolstering behavioural patterns so that they might better navigate the male dominated world in which they lived. But Stanley and Compton, especially Maude

Stanley, approached the task from a place of collusion with that world. Neither one challenged it. In the 1960s the world was barely any easier for young women to navigate than it had been at the time of the opening of the Theatre Girls' Club in 1915 Then, life for women was rigidly prescriptive as law-makers, men of varying degrees of privilege, rendered the society they fashioned almost perfectly blind to women's lives. A place like the Theatre Girls' Club was a boon to the young women who stayed there because it was a place distinct from all that went on beyond its walls. It was a place for them.

59 Greek Street had also been a place of sanctuary to Agnes Bell. In 1964 Miss Bell turned eighty and her retirement could not be put off. In that year the matter was settled; she retired from her post as warden and secretary of the Theatre Girls' Club in the following January. 59 Greek Street had been her home for some forty years. The change would have been a great wrench to her. 'The Club is to make a presentation to Miss Bell as a simple expression of the gratitude of so many over these years,' wrote Compton Mackenzie in *The Stage* on 1st April 1965. 'There are records of no less than 5000 girls who have stayed at the Club during Miss Bell's period... and I am sure there are many who would welcome the opportunity of joining in this testimonial.'

One who did was the singer Anna Pollak whose time at the club was in the 1930s. Her letter was printed in *The Stage* on 14th January 1965:[177]

> I am sure thousands of "Old Girls" like myself who were once young girls at the Theatre Girls' Club would like to join me in a tribute of gratitude and good wishes to Miss Agnes Bell who has been its warden and secretary for the past thirty-seven years and, coincidentally with her colleague and near-neighbour Miss Molly Howell of the Interval Club, retires

this month. Selflessly and without publicity Miss Bell has been guardian, adviser and friend to countless girls coming to London to rehearse, train or look for work, many of them really in need of care and protection. Her sympathy, tolerance and common-sense were as inexhaustible as bed and board were spare. Vivid are the memories of those recurring unrewarding tramps from one audition or agent to another being followed by a surprise invitation to tea and sympathy in Miss Bell's bed-sitter at the top of the house, or being taken as an out-of-work treat to one of the Soho cafes...for coffee and eclairs, or into the Club cellar to be given a string of beads, a fan or some romantic curio from her basket of stage props. As the only residential hostel of its kind, the TGC continues to do a unique job, but the gap she leaves will never be filled because its unusual character and pattern of life, practically unaltered since its foundation by Mrs Edward Compton, have been sustained by dauntless, dedicated Aggie Bell.

Molly Hewett of the Interval Club retired at the same time as Agnes Bell, and with her retirement came the closure of the Interval Club. At the retirement of Agnes Bell in 1965, the Theatre Girls' Club experienced a revival. The board arranged for an overhaul of the club's appearance, its rules and constitution. As to Miss Bell, she spent a short time in the popular seaside town of Troon in Scotland. Perhaps she had gone there as a child with her parents and thought it a good place for retirement.[178] She must have changed her mind, because she returned to England to live in Winchester.

In July 1965 the Theatre Girls' Club was registered as a charity under the title '59 Greek Street Limited', by which the articles of association negotiated in 1935 underwent amendment. Its objective, really no different from Virginia Compton's in 1915, was:

> to provide a home with board and lodging for impoverished girls or women who may be employed or are seeking employment in the theatrical, music hall, or filming professions or any other occupation connected with the stage. To provide social and recreational facilities for residents with a view to improving their conditions of life and to give financial aid to any impoverished girl who may be employed in the profession.[179]

Marilyn Rogers, who had stayed at the club in 1962, paid a visit not long after the club's reinvention in 1965. 'What a change. The dorms were now bright rooms with chintz bedspreads where several girls sat chatting and laughing. In the lounge downstairs a guy sat with his girlfriend and a male photographer was welcomed in! I wasn't staying there but I don't think the ghost was either!'[180]

So, the hospital-like atmosphere of the cubicles, the 'horse-boxes', was gone. In came 1960s light wood beds with matching bedside cabinet and mirror, floral patterned curtains at the windows. The building's decor was lightened, the dark wood panelling spoken of just five years earlier was either removed or made to seem less oppressive. The beautiful stone stair with iron balusters of the 1883 building was still there sweeping upwards from the hallway to the first floor and old music room. These cheerful renovations at the Theatre Girls' Club took place beside life's dark and tragic side, which is how it was in Soho. The feted boxer Freddie Mills was found dead in Goslett Yard, just one roof-top to the east of the club, on 25th July 1965. Doubt remains as to whether he committed suicide or was murdered by local gangsters.

The Theatre Girls' Club was re-opened in July 1966 by Vanessa Redgrave who called it 'a smashing place.'[181] A new supervisor was found, one of a long line of women who, since the days of Maude Stanley's Club & Home for Working Girls, had overseen the daily lives of those who lodged at No 59. Ursula Peters, a woman who had nursed soldiers on the Western Front during World War II, came to the Theatre Girls' Club as replacement to Miss Bell and with her came a far more relaxed approach to the club's running. The Theatre Girls' Club entered a kind of golden period under the wardenship of Mrs Peters. Prospective boarders still had to fill in an application form, parental approval was expected, a signing in and out book was retained along with the curfew, extended to 11 p.m. But the ban on male visitors was slowly relaxed and residents were treated as responsible adults.

Joy Clarkson *(from Exeter, 1965, aged 16)*

> I recall the sheer relief of this safe haven in the midst of the perils of Soho in London's 'swinging 60s'! I was a young dancer of just sixteen setting out on the rocky road of show biz, auditioning for musicals, summer seasons and pantomimes. Theatre Girls' was a warm and welcoming place where a strict rule was implemented that all thick curtains must, at all times, be tightly drawn so that we girls could come to breakfast, bleary-eyed in dressing gowns against the prying eyes of would be predators lurking in Greek Street!

However, this rule was broken (slightly) in the early hours of a Saturday morning when the ladies of the night would come into the street for their cat fights. We would rise from our cosy dormitory beds and peep through the drapes, wide-eyed at the display below. A couple of times I witnessed the heated brawls between the ladies culminated in clumps of hair being extracted, and the language was more colourful than a drunken bunch of sailors but nonetheless extremely entertaining. I vividly remember 3 girls who used to go to bed right after dinner, put their alarms on for a few hours later, get up, apply some slap, leave in the dead of night and visit wealthy young Arabs in an exclusive West End Club and then onto who knows . . ! I think they returned in the early hours and went right onto school.

There was a common room for guests but I never ventured in there myself. At 16 I felt quite overawed by these rather eccentric students some of which attended RADA, And there was a strict signing in and out book overseen by a protective German lady, whose name I can't recall. I took to her immediately. She had a small office where she would be known to indulge in a tipple or two! Nevertheless, she kept a tight ship! Dancers in particular are always hungry. Only once did I lose my appetite when one of the girls rushed in, tossing off her fur coat on the floor and, whilst gobbling down her meal, relayed an incident which had just happened a few paces away. Apparently, a man with a knife in his back was pushed from a doorway in Greek Street, falling at her feet. "I had to walk right over him" she said!

During the day, Soho was a novel place to be. I was hassled but this seemed to be perfectly normal to me then. In those heady days Sunday shopping was practically non-existent, so we would often stroll to the friendly Jewish delicatessens and buy delicious pastries. They closed on a Saturday due to the Sabbath. It wasn't always a peaceful stroll; sometimes we ran the gauntlet from the "Pimps" in the doorways who would try to entice us in. My closest friend at the time was an outrageous 15 year old from Canada who used to wear shaggy fur coats and took delight in bad mouthing the prostitutes!! One of our girls would regularly spit at them and we would have to race back, in hysterics to the safety of the Theatre Girls' Club and draw the curtains tight!

I worked as a professional dancer in summer shows and pantomimes for the Bernard Delfont/Grade organisation. There was a long run in the Danny La Rue show in London's West End – Prince of Wales Theatre. There was touring and TVs. Latterly, I choreographed and then took up the reins of Stagecoach Principal, running several schools in Truro. I bought a Stagecoach School in Exmouth and sold it on retirement.

Carole Harvey *(later Fripp, from Southend-on-Sea, stayed in 1966)*

I went to Bush Davies Theatre School in 1962, then for the next three or four years did pantos and summer seasons with Martin Shaw, Leslie Crowther, Sid James and Kenneth Connor, Roy Hudd and Mark Wynter, Danny la Rue and

Ronnie Corbett. My friend Sylvia and I were in digs at Battersea when we arranged to stay at the Theatre Girls' Club in 1966. We moved there because our Battersea landlady was fierce and one weekend when I was at my parents Sylvia had a man to stay! Remember this was the 60s. The woman told everyone what terrible girls we were and threw us out.

Every dancer knew about the Theatre Girls' Club. Our show was at Lyons Corner House and the Club's location was convenient. The club's manageress greeted us and showed us around. She was a Polish lady. We stayed in an upstairs room and the facilities were adequate. We were used to the West End and were never hassled in Soho. Even though we were working, a necessary way of life was to go to classes at the Dance Centre in Floral Street and Max Rivers studios and to hang about to find out gossip and the latest shows coming to town and who would choreograph, and of course the auditions. To get extra money I used to sometimes dress the chorus at the Palace Theatre or switch the house light on and off at the Apollo Theatre. This involved sitting on a hard tiny seat and watching The Beggar's Opera. These jobs were matinees only as in the evening we were dancing in the Showboat Cabaret at Trafalgar Square.

We didn't find the club's curfew oppressive – we were exhausted and glad to relax. It was a time of the club scene, great fashions and wonderful music. Except for *The Stage* I didn't read a paper or watch the news! There were a few Tiller Girls staying at the Theatre Girls' Club who I joined for a summer season in 1967. Sylvia had a bad case of bed bugs while we were at the Theatre Girls' Club which made us decide to commute home to Essex for the remainder of the Showboat run. I was back with the Tillers in '68/9, worked at the Casino de Paris then in 1969-70 in South Africa. Then I married and taught at a dance school and choreographed for school and public events until, in the 1980s I bought my own dance school.

It looks as though a good number of ex-Theatre Girls' Club residents turned to teaching after marriage.

In 1967 the lease on 59 Greek Street was renewed for another twenty-one years at a rent of £1,000 per annum under terms allowing the lessor, the London Union of Youth Clubs, seven yearly reviews. For the entirety of August that year the club was closed. As soon as it opened again, sixteen-year-old Jenny Morton came to stay.

Jenny Morton *(later Dunster, from Sheffield, stayed 1967 and 1968, age 16)*

> I left Bush Davies at 16 at end of Easter term to go to the Andrew Hardie Ballet School in South Kensington then stayed with family friends in North London for the summer term. The Theatre Girls' Club was on a list provided by the Andrew Hardie School along with various YWCA hostels which we also looked at but weren't keen. My mother never really wanted me to go on the stage and did everything to discourage me and her eyes nearly fell out of her head when she saw where the Theatre Girls' Club was situated. My parents booked me in at the Theatre Girls' Club and paid

them. The TGC was much more friendly and social than the YWCA hostels and at that time I think it had been recently redecorated and looked a lot better. Also there were many others in the same position as myself who had left schools such as Bush Davies, Elmhurst and the boarding part of Arts Educational, so we all had something in common. Most of the girls I met there were really nice. Also TGC provided dinner which the YWCA didn't and I certainly wasn't savvy enough to feed myself. The food wasn't that brilliant but at least it was there.

I was greeted by the lady who was the manager who may have been German. I can't remember her name; however I recall that I liked her and she treated us all as adults and organised the odd social occasion in the first floor lounge when we could invite friends, male and female. There was also an older lady who was a full-time resident who I think was called Rosemary and worked for Equity who also showed us the ropes. I stayed there during 1967 and 1968 and occasionally when I was rehearsing for a show. I shared a dormitory with other girls who were at Arts Education at Hyde Park Corner most of the time. I loved it and it was in such a perfect position. I learned a lot by chatting to some of the professional performers, garnering tips that stood me in a good stead for my early first auditions and shows.

Greek Street was a bit of a shock at first although I had walked through the area several times before when visiting London with my parents. I do know that at the time the Maltese Mafia were in charge of all the strip clubs and girls, and that there were a lot of turf wars around. However, most of the establishments knew who we were by sight and made sure that we weren't hassled by men using their clubs. The doormen at the clubs closest to the TGC knew a lot of us by sight and warned their punters off. I remember a couple of times when they sort of actively came to my rescue. There was a curfew for us younger ones of 11.00 pm I think, and we were always finding ways to get round it. I used to sneak out to the Marquee Club in Wardour Street to see all the greats like Eric Clapton, Jimi Hendrix, Cream, [and] often came through the little side streets and never really felt threatened.

I think we were protected in the nicest possible way. We had our freedom during non-curfew times to come and go, and friends could visit us for coffee in the first floor lounge. No-one asked where you'd been and where you were going. I remember many a Saturday night going to a party somewhere then sleeping on the floor until the first tube on a Sunday morning and sneaking back in during breakfast time past the manager's office. However, I was so green that the TGC was a perfect safe haven for me to stay in. I do recall a couple of times I sort of found myself in dubious situations that I was able to get out of by mentioning the curfew and that people would be looking for me.

I worked as a professional dancer for people like Lionel Blair, Pamela Davis and Irving Davies in the theatre, TV, cabaret and corporate shows. My first job was in Gt Yarmouth as a Pamela Davis dancer with Morecombe and Wise and my last as a dancer was for the BBC in the famous

117

Angela Rippon kicking line on the Morecombe and Wise Christmas Special. In 1977 or thereabout I started an agency called Razzamatazz Management and Productions with Jill Shirley in the West End for dancers and musical theatre people. We became one of the biggest dance agencies of the time and were part of the team that created Bucks Fizz for Eurovision. I went on to have my own agency Whatever Artists Management in 1996 which I still do on a low key basis, amongst other things working with dancers from Strictly Come Dancing and representing my old 'boss' Lionel Blair.

I loved my time at the TGC and still from time to time walk past the building and think fondly of it. It was the perfect place for me to stay at that time in my life and of course there was no-one looking down their noses at 'these dreadful show business types.' I really don't think that these days there is a need for this type of digs and I don't think that it would make any difference to the claims made by the 'Me Too' generation. In the 60s life was very different. There was no equality at all and the casting couch was very prevalent I seem to recall. (I know I picked up loads of tips on how to handle myself in the big world while at the TGC.) But nowadays no-one can hide from social media.

And so, although the 1960s were still early days in terms of social change, it was now that the relationship between the sexes began to shift. Sexual activity became more overt and this had much to do with ready contraception for women, legalised for married women in 1961 then extended to single women in 1967.   Birth control had always been viewed 'with a sort of horror,' wrote Bertrand Russell in 1967.[182]   In fact it had been considered a vice.   Back in 1877 Annie Besant and Charles Bradlaugh had been prosecuted for promoting contraception as a solution to the problems of too large families, at the very time that Maude Stanley was promoting, albeit obscurely, the ideas of Malthus and Ruskin.   In the 1960s, common sense conquered. Contraception became a social good and not merely because of the avoidance of untimely pregnancies. Women now began to feel more in control of their sexuality and their bodies, and thereby their place in society.

Also significant was that young people found their voice and became a force to be reckoned with. They saw corruption and vested interest in the corridors of power and spoke against it.   The profoundly shocked response to an image taken by photographer Eddie Adam of the summary killing of Viet Cong officer Nguyễn Văn Lém was youth demonstrations against the Vietnam War. Demonstrations against war were novel. In Britain, limited national conscription had ended only eight years earlier. Young men had queued up to go to war fifty years earlier, now they and young women were protesting against it.

However, at the Theatre Girls' Club, politics did not impinge too deeply. Your author was staying at the club in this year and can attest to it. The young performers there remained focused on their next job and things went on at the club much as they always had. Theatre censorship ended in September 1968 and the show *Hair*, depicting youth's anti-war counterculture and sexual liberation opened at the Shaftesbury Theatre on 27th September. At least one at the club did play her part in the theatrical representation of this decade's social revolution. Anabel Littledale came to the club in 1969 when she was fifteen years old to play in *Hair*.

Anabel Littledale *(from Hampton, stayed 1969, age 15)*

I was in *Hair* at the time. I loved living at the Theatre Girls' Club... so exciting living in Soho. Me, being under sixteen, the Theatre Girls' Club was a safe place – which it certainly was. We had a 10 p.m. curfew and Soho was full of pimps and prostitutes. A real red-light district but because we were at the Theatre Girls' Club all those people who were on the street, all those regular people, would really look out for us, so we probably didn't really walk home alone from the theatre. Some of the girls [at the club] were pretty gorgeous – we had some of the Blue Bell girls there, beautiful dancers, actresses, but the [Greek Street] bouncers, even the prostitutes were really looking out for us, making sure that we got home and nobody harassed us, so in a sense we got right into the heart of this life in Greek Street.

We lived in dormitories. I remember Debby Lavin, a little older than me, we connected immediately. She took me under her wing and she seemed to be very much in the know as to who was who, what we could do – she was a very free spirit, not bound by anybody and she could out-talk anybody... so that's how a lot of my time was spent. We were pretty busy, all in shows of some kind. We were working in the evenings, in the day time just cooling out, maybe shopping together but mainly we were preparing for the next show.

I do remember how noisy it was at night because there was so much action [on the street] but only when it was summertime and we had to have the windows open would we hear the real humdinging kind of arguments... We also had access to the most wonderful Indian restaurants. There was the Ronnie Scott's Club and I remember seeing Peter Sarstedt and it was great. We were living really like adults but we were protected adults and we were having a lot of fun. Sometimes we had to run up against the strict matron but I don't ever remember that being a real problem.

The Theatre Girls' Club was a very welcome place and my family was very pleased that I had a safe place to be because being in the theatre there were lots of parties after the show. You couldn't always sleep after doing a show so it was really fun to have all the girls there, we would all just laugh and giggle before falling off to sleep. It was very clean, very well run. I had no complaints about it. It was very wholesome and I don't remember any arguments with anyone. I was really under Debby's wing. We did an awful lot of things together during the day and Debby became a life-long friend.

I think I did some other work during the time I was in *Hair* because there was a lot of PR work. I had a solo song in the show and then I auditioned for the Eurovision Song Contest. A manager approached me and said "I'd really like to work with you and develop you and make you into a star" as they all say, but I had to sign this contract and the conditions that he gave me were that I basically couldn't get married, I couldn't even have a boyfriend for five years. When I saw that kind of commitment I really wasn't ready for it, so that was how I entertained other things.

Soon after this I had a strong knee injury and operation. Then I fell madly in love and the fellow I met, he wanted me to go and live with him in Canada, travel with him and be with him. It was the 60s, the 70s. We were experimenting with things, so I left.

Deborah Lavin, Anabel Littledale's friend at the club, was one boarder who was politically aware and in later life wrote and spoke on Victorian politics, secularism, a free press, slavery, prostitution. She had attended Corona Theatre School in Hammersmith for a short while and found her way to the Theatre Girls' Club in 1968 when she was seventeen. 'I arrived in February 1968, a friend of my mother Kay Lyell who used to be a Mother Goose arranged it for me (and that is a story in itself)... There were a couple of girls at Murrays when I was there, they suggested I go and wait table there, I declined so I never saw inside it.'[183] According to one who worked at Murray's night club on Beak Street, the hostesses were fined if they were late, also for having laddered stockings and for having bruises.[184] Another boarder in 1968 was Liz Dallas Ross, a RADA stage management student who went on to work on Mike Leigh's early productions. Dancer, Carol Sagar, also boarded at the club in the late '60s.

Carol Sagar *(from Felixstowe, 1969, age 16)*

I came to the Theatre Girls' Club in early May 1969 from my parents' home in Felixstowe, Suffolk. I always wanted to be a dancer from the time I started age 6. I auditioned for the summer season in 1969 with Bunny Baron at Clacton-on-Sea, Westcliffe Theatre. I remember when my contract came I was appearing in a local amateur production of Calamity Jane and my parents brought it to show me. It felt fantastic, I was on my way. I heard about the Theatre Girls' Club from my dancing teacher, Margot Spencer. My parents were terrified about me going to London and living in a place so near Soho. It was alien to them as I have been the first in our family to have a career in show business. My father couldn't come to terms with the fact that I was only on half pay for rehearsals, a sum of £6 a week and the cost of the Theatre Girls' Club was £9 for the week. It doesn't seem much now but it was a lot then. But my parents organised my stay at the Club and my father paid for me.

The Theatre Girls' Club was typical of its time, clean and a bit utility but OK. When I first arrived I remember a lady coming out of an office on the right, greeting us and showing us to my room and saying I couldn't have a key as I wasn't 17 – it might have been 18. I was only there about 10 days, rehearsing at the Concert Artistes Association in Bedford Street on the Strand for the summer show for Bunny Baron Productions. I remember getting the tube and going the wrong way, only once though. On my first day I went back to the club for lunch but after that I stayed with the other girls and we went to the Wimpey Bar – all the rage then.

The Theatre Girls' Club was definitely somewhere safe to be and having the meal at night was great, no idea what we ate though. All the girls I met there were really nice. I was in awe of many of them as they were tall showgirls from probably Talk of the Town, the height of sophistication to me. I definitely felt safer at the club than I would have elsewhere.

Greek Street was exciting, I had no problems but I didn't really walk around as we were rehearsing all day and I stayed in at night so I didn't mind the curfew because I was too shattered after rehearsals. I just stayed in my room after dinner.

I did a few seasons as a dancer and they found out I had a good singing voice, so they gave me some solos to sing. No extra money mind you. When I became a principal singer there was no pay for rehearsals until Equity brought in the minimum rate, and you had to provide your own tights and shoes. Then I decided to pursue a singing career, which I did, doing holiday centres, visiting cabaret, northern clubs, summer seasons as soubrette, musicals and then cruising.

I think places like the Theatre Girls' Club are a good thing. It's a community that you belong to which is no bad thing.

PART VI
1970-2020

10

The Building's Reinvention: theatre girls to the homeless

Compton Mackenzie, now Sir Compton Mackenzie, resigned as president of the Theatre Girls' Club in the New Year of 1970. He was eight-seven years old, almost blind and ready to leave London for retirement in Edinburgh.[185] Harry Secombe took over as president. Within twelve months of Compton Mackenzie's retirement, the Theatre Girls' Club ceased its traditional role as a home-from-home to young women working in the theatre.

Harry Secombe visited the club one sunny afternoon in the spring of 1970. Your author was there for the occasion. Mrs Peters gathered together what boarders she could and we arrayed ourselves by the club room piano to be regaled by his warm good humour. I doubt any of us had but the vaguest notion of why he was there. I worked with Harry Secombe two or three times in later years and could so easily have asked him what was behind the change of use at 59 Greek Street, why the club closed its doors to young dancers and actors. Had I known then that I would be writing the story of the Theatre Girls' Club fifty years later I could have learned the details of its demise from one who knew it better than any. Early in 1971 the Theatre Girls' Club closed, and in the June of that year Agnes Bell, witness to most of what had happened at 59 Greek Street during the club's fifty-four-year tenure, died at Winchester.

Perhaps the modest and slowly shifting perceptions of woman's place in society, which entered a new phase in the 1960s, had something to do with the decision to close the Theatre Girls' Club, but those social changes were slight, still very much in their infancy, barely felt. Perhaps it simply floundered when there was no Compton family member to keep it going as there had been from its founding in 1914. The club's closure within a few months of Compton Mackenzie's resignation as its president can hardly be unconnected. Very likely, lack of funding was a major cause of the closure of the Theatre Girls' Club in 1971. The club had relied financially upon its own investments in the early years together with fund-raising exercises by family and friends. A low rent, largely thanks to Lady Carlisle had also helped. There was money in the mid-60s to refurbish the club but within eighteen months of the retirement of Compton Mackenzie in 1970, the building stood empty. The Theatre Girls' Club committee continued on though, for many years more.

The discovery, as it were, of homelessness in the late-1960s might have played a part in the club's closure. Jeremy Sandford's play *Cathy Come Home* shocked viewers when it was first televised in 1966. It charted in uncompromising detail a young couple's decline into homelessness and was, in its way, a moment when art changed the world. In the year of the first broadcast of *Cathy Come Home,* campaigning charities for the homeless were founded: Shelter, Crisis, and Christian Action. The same had happened after W. T. Stead's exposé of the sex trade in children back in 1885. Then the National Vigilance Association and the Jewish Association for the Protection of Women and Girls had been formed in direct response. After *Cathy Come Home,* the daily press began to carry articles on homelessness. It was estimated that there were over ten thousand homeless in the London area.[186] Numbers might or might not have increased on previous years but concerns about homelessness and the nation's mental health had. One member of parliament wrote in 1970:

Looking back on my constituency case work since the war, I am struck by the fall in the number of problems caused by external factors, while the number of problems caused by the constituent's personality difficulties has increased. I know that many of my colleagues in the House have been struck the same way... nothing is solved by simply providing jobs, homes or grants of money.'[187]

Concern over poor mental health, homelessness and their connection was a mighty change from the focus of Maude Stanley and her male social-worker-in-arms Henry Solly one hundred years earlier. Stanley and Solly had provided clubs and improving activities to any who showed promise and willingness to join their circumscribed society. Addressing vagrancy and abject poverty, in other words helping those in the direst need and considered beyond rehabilitation, had not been their objective.[188] By the early-1970s it was a consuming concern. The concentration of government bodies and charitable organisations turned to the spectre of thousands of homeless and mentally traumatised people who had always been there but, on the whole, had been given up as helpless by these well-connected bodies and organisations until now. The needs of healthy young women keen to come to London to seek fame and fortune in the theatre, in television or film, or indeed any other business, were over-shadowed by it. Such a shift of focus clearly played a part in the Theatre Girls' Club committee's decision to invite Christian Action to take over 59 Greek Street in 1971.[189]

Christian Action, formed by a group of London churches in 1966 at the time of the *Cathy Come Home* broadcast, opened a refuge for women in 1967 at

12 Lambeth High Street. By 1971 the Lambeth refuge had slept more than one thousand women and the need was growing. It was receiving grants from the Supplementary Benefits Commission and Home Office amounting to some £16,000 a year, the latter through an After-Care and Probation Hostels Grant for ex-offenders. Demand upon the refuge was far greater than capacity so when the Theatre Girls' Club proposed that Christian Action take over 59 Greek Street, Christian Action's Projects Officer, Nicholas Beacock, met the idea with enthusiasm: 'in conjunction with the TGC,' he said, 'it will be possible to run the first comprehensive project for homeless people in the British Isles.' 'We need these beds. They need our grant. We still need another reception centre for women in London,' wrote another.[190]

David Brandon, a thirty-year-old psychiatric social worker and recent recruit from local government, acted as Christian Action's manager at 59 Greek Street. He did not much like the building. 'It was institutionally designed, and had an old Edwardian gentlemen's club atmosphere, both entirely inappropriate to its new purpose,' he wrote.'[191] His impression of the building says something about Maude Stanley's concept of her Club & Home for Working Girls, and much about David Brandon, who was strongly averse to anything smacking of charity-with-an-agenda which he distinctly identified as a Victorian mode surviving into the 1960s:

> Churches ran missions on the Embankment to save the souls
> of the lost and fallen. Men stood singing hymns in the rain
> and were given a meat sandwich and a mug of steaming tea
> for their pains. Some winos boasted of being 'converted'
> twenty or thirty times. It was the easiest way of getting a new
> suit, money in your pocket and somewhere to sleep. Prodigal
> sons were always welcome.[192]

Prodigal daughters began to be welcomed too. They were welcomed into 59 Greek Street when it opened in November 1971 as Christian Action's flagship initiative towards alleviating women's homelessness.

The Lambeth refuge grants were transferred into the hands of a combined management of Christian Action's subsidiary Homeless in Britain and the Theatre Girls' Club committee. 59 Greek Street would never again function as it had for the past ninety years, first as a place of improvement for working girls and young women then as a home in London for young dancers, singers and actors. Now it was a place for women who manifestly had not realised their youthful dreams but had found themselves thrown up upon the shores of life's most vicious seas.

The project at 59 Greek Street was David Brandon's first with Christian Action. He took over Ursula Peter's old room at the top of the first flight of stairs and, probably without knowing it, became the first man to sleep at 59 Greek Street. 'Some of the staff thought the new building was much too big and impersonal' he wrote, and some shared his fears about running an institutional project.'[193] Yet, so young and radical-thinking a man as David Brandon was capable of falling into gender biased judgement. He thought the very saddest of homeless people were the women: 'A home and a woman seem to go so much together,' he wrote, 'and a homeless woman seems to lose all human dignity.'[194]

Rosemary, whose surname is not given, was the first woman to move into 59 Greek Street after the closure of the Theatre Girls' Club. She came from the Lambeth refuge in November 1971 and was soon joined by the rest of the women staying there. They did not like their new location. 59 Greek Street could sleep more than forty while the Lambeth refuge was a small terraced house for fourteen. From the start No 59 was 'overwhelmed with violence [and] shook with anxiety,' wrote David Brandon.[195] A good many of the women were alcohol or drug addicted and suffered dreadfully from emotional or psychiatric problems. Rosemary was diagnosed as a depressed intropunitive, aggressive psychopath. She said her early life had been so bad that she had had to invent another one.[196]

As time went on, neither resident nor staff found 59 Greek Street a congenial place to be. 'It's filthy here nowadays', said one. 'The place is simply diabolical.'[197] There were 'pushes, punches, split and bloody heads. Crockery and windows broken; chairs smashed.' There were drug overdoses, 'slashed wrists and faces.'[198] David Brandon was threatened by a resident wielding a carving knife. All this within a few months of the Theatre Girls' Club's closure. Now the House of Charity and its neighbour, the Gay Hussar (formerly the Budapest public house) were witnessing regular arrivals of ambulance and police vehicles across the street from them. In all of Greek Street's history, this was a level of dysfunction not seen before.

Christian Action's management team fully understood that the working staff at No 59 'despite their enthusiasm and sense of commitment, are themselves very vulnerable because of their inexperience and lack of skill and knowledge.'[199] Within 59 Greek Street was a staff of six, Pamela Thompson, Elizabeth Bailey, Martin Guedalla, Veronica Held, Martin Housden and Kate Poulton, giving twenty-four-hour cover. They had no leader but instead worked on an equal partnership basis. Their policy was to let people be.

The ninety-year-old building was showing signs of severe stress too. Some repair and adaptation to 59 Greek Street was carried out at this time. Perhaps it is now that the fine stone spandrel staircase, with its iron handrail and balusters, upon which aristocratic visitors had made their way upwards to the old music room, and where boarders had chosen to sit during WWII bombing raids, was removed and probably sold. Amanda Barrie entered the building in 2008 by which time the 'fabulous Victorian interior' which she remembered from the '40s and '50s, was gone.[200]

59 Greek Street's landlord was still the London Union of Youth Clubs working from St Anne's House in Venn Street, Clapham. The Union's Chief Executive, Harvey Hinds, was also chief whip of the Greater London Council Labour group. The Union did not like what was going on at No 59. Under the 1966 lease signed by the, then, newly refurbished Theatre Girls' Club, the Union could review the rent every seven years and this is exactly what it did. In 1973 the London Union of Youth Clubs contested in court the use of the building under Christian Action's Homeless in Britain management and sought re-possession. The outcome was that Christian Action was allowed to stay at 59 Greek Street on condition that a yearly rent of £5,000 was paid. This was a five-fold increase on the rent set in 1966. The relationship between lessor and lessee never improved.

More difficulties presented themselves when, in 1976, Homeless in Britain's primary funder the Supplementary Benefits Commission, gave notice that the 'Theatre Girls' Club' project, which was providing long-term stays, even 'permanent accommodation', did not satisfy their new guidelines.[201] They could give grants to short-term settlements only. There were plenty of women staying at 59 Greek Street for only a week or two at a time, but some had lived there for up to five years, paying from £19 to £21 a week for full board and lodging, met by the Department of Health and Social Security. Nonetheless, the Commission began gradually to withdraw its funding so that over the next two years it fell from £13,000 in 1975 to £5,000 in 1977. This was a blow that Homeless in Britain's management team, working from a second-floor office at 357 The Strand, found impossible to overcome. In 1977 they split from Christian Action to form Homeless Action and Accommodation while continuing in amalgamation with the Theatre Girls' Club management to provide the service at 59 Greek Street.[202] David Brandon had been gone some time by now to take up work elsewhere.

Things at 59 Greek Street struggled on. In 1978 a documentary film called *Theatre Girls* was made by Kim Longinotto, then a student at the National Film and Television School, and Claire Pollak of what was going on inside 59 Greek Street. *Time Out* said of it:

> Down in Soho's Greek Street is the Theatre Girls Club, a dilapidated hostel for homeless single women. This stark documentary picture of some of its occupants by National Film School students allows the women (many were in the theatre, and are delightfully, painfully extroverted) to tell their own story; humour and self-deprecating irony are punctuated by moments of aggression, tenderness, and sheer, terrifying isolation. There's not enough analysis: of the reasons the women are there; of why their 'open door' refuge is so pitifully under-subsidised; or, ultimately, of the film's own motives. But it does present a shocking vision of largely middle-aged, frustrated losers, their minds often addled by drink or drugs, their fantasies injected with the harshest self-knowledge. Not a film recommended if you're already depressed, but one which ought to make you think.[203]

Among the women who stayed at 59 Greek Street during these years was seventy-three-year-old Phyllis, one of those who had come from the Lambeth refuge in 1971. Born into a middle-class family, she had trained as a nurse then, for reasons unknown, ended up sleeping rough and drinking meths. She was still able bodied and throve on the companionship of the other women. Others were more disturbed. One twenty-five-year-old had 'formidable problems beyond anything the Theatre Girls' Club' can reasonably provide.'[204] When pregnant her husband had abandoned her. Her child had been taken into care. She had been injured in a pub bombing, imprisoned for theft and now was violent and self-harming. Another woman was 'distressed and distressing to others,' and yet did, early in 1978 and by some miracle, manage to get herself to a clinic in Geneva where she said she had 'escaped from England.' She was deported back home after being diagnosed with triple schizophrenia.

March 1978, and the dire plight of Theatre Girls' Club finances came to a head. And yet 59 Greek Street was full, every bed taken. On one night of duty Pamela Thompson had to turn four destitute women away from the door. And she was concerned with the physical nursing carried out at No 59 by untrained carers. 'In the course of nature,' she told a Homeless Action and Accommodation meeting 'the women over 60 will weaken and die' and in order for staff 'to be able to handle this situation it [is] justifiable to undergo a practical crash course in basic nursing.' Such was the situation at 59 Greek Street. When closure threatened, one of the management team, Helen Austerberry, said it would leave 'at least 60 women with nowhere to go.'[205]

Closure of the reception centre at No 59 continued to threaten, but Home Office and Westminster City Council officials, faced with having to turn out onto the street women suffering from debilitating low self-esteem, drug and alcohol addiction and mental illness, conceded that 'money must be put into Greek Street to keep it going.'[206] Within three weeks of these Home Office and Westminster City Council's assurances of continued funding, Helen Austerberry received a letter from Greater London Council dated 14th April 1978, telling her it was 'not possible that Council funds be put into the renewal of these premises.'[207] A proportion of the agencies involved seemed to want the problem of homeless women simply to go away. At much the same time, the then Labour Secretary of State for Social Services is recorded to have said that alcoholism in men 'is crude and embarrassing. In women, it's plain sickening.'[208] So much, then, for gender parity. Echoes here of the attitudes prevailing in Maude Stanley's time.

1978 saw talks continuing between the combined management of Homeless Action and Accommodation and the Theatre Girls' Club with the three main funding agencies, Greater London Council, the Home Office, and various departments of Westminster City Council, in an attempt to shore-up finances. No 59's management team explained why the project had fallen into a deficit exceeding £10,000. Lack of accurate financial projections (including budgeting for doctors' visits, solicitor and bank charges), a failure to reach an 85% rent collection, and the 'lack of response from or appeals to grant aiding bodies'[209] The Supplementary Benefits Commission, which had been slowly withdrawing its funding from the scheme, was asked to review its decision. These talks held off what was sure to come. The reception centre for women at No 59 lingered on for a while longer.

59 Greek Street was now a 'rambling, dilapidated' place.[210] There were cockroaches and other vermin about. It was estimated that £28,000 was needed just to meet fire precaution requirements. Early in 1979 the insulation plates at the base of the kitchen's old gas range failed. The floorboards beneath were found smouldering. There was a burst water pipe and some of the old lead piping had to be replaced. The roof needed to be repaired, skylights were leaking. Letters were sent to the lessors, London

Union of Youth Clubs, asking for repairs to be made. There was no response.

This is the last that is heard of Homeless Action and Accommodation's operations at 59 Greek Street, at least from records at the National Archives at Kew. What is known is that the women were moved out of 59 Greek Street and homeless men were moved in. For the first time in its one-hundred-year history the building raised by Maude Stanley in 1883 was welcoming men through its doors. Throughout the 1980s, 1990s and into the 2000s, 59 Greek Street continued to provide a roof over the heads of the homeless. Soho Housing Association acquired No 59 in 1998 when Centrepoint, the charity affiliated to Soho's St Anne's Church, ran the last scheme to provide accommodation for the homeless in the building, this time for young people: 59 Greek Street never lost sight of its original purpose. The Centrepoint scheme closed in 2014 because of lack of funding. Two years later, Westminster Council gave provisional permission to Soho Housing for the building to be commercially developed. Work to remove the internal walls of 59 Greek Street and to convert the one-hundred-and-thirty-four-year-old building into apartments and commercial space began in January 2017.

For nearly one hundred years, from 1883 until the close of the 1970s, 59 Greek Street was a place dedicated to women. Today, it offers apartments at affordable rents and penthouse accommodation on the top floor at commercial rates. Maude Stanley's gymnasium and music room are now but a memory. The ground floor dining room and basement rehearsal room from the days of the Theatre Girls' Club are retail units. Virginia Compton's rooms are gone, her chapel is gone. The laundry room on the top floor, where young dancers just back from tour in 1937 washed their clothes and where Margaret Dobson and Mary Wylie comforted themselves with cups of warmed Ambrosia milk in 1948, is a penthouse bathroom or bedroom. 59 Greek Street has been restored and reinvented under the wing of Soho Housing Association; its walls still provide affordable living to people working in central London.

An entity known as The Theatre Girls' Club survived from 1914 until 28th October 1998 which was the day on which the Charity Commission recorded that it ceased to exist. For fifty-four years, 59 Greek Street was home to the Theatre Girls' Club. Thousands of resilient young women passed along its corridors, climbed up and down its stairs, sat in its club room, chatted in its dining room, and practiced dance and song from its top to its bottom. A seeming majority enjoyed their time there, some of us appreciate it to this day. 59 Greek Street has sheltered the most hopeful and the most helpless which is a legacy of inestimable and lasting value.

AUTHOR'S POSTSCRIPT

Deborah Lavin, Anabel Littledale, Liz Dallas Ross and I stayed together at the Theatre Girls' Club between 1968 and 1970. I thought of the club as my main address in those days. Having since read more than two decades-worth of recollections of the club, 1943 to 1967, it's clear that our stays were longer than most. Dancers, making up the majority of boarders, came-and-went because most were rehearsing for British or overseas tours, while the few of us who were actors (in Liz's case a student stage-manager) were often looking for work or already working in the West End, so we were as good as permanent residents at the club and enjoyed the privilege. The club functioned only as a residence in our time. There were no activities taking place as there had been in Virginia Compton's day. During the 1920s classes were available to residents and non-residents but exactly when this tradition ended isn't known. Audrey Crockett, who stayed at the club in 1944, says there were no classes then and thinks they probably ended during the Second World War.

Soho was the greatest place in London to live. It took you in and wrapped you up and offered everything London had to give. It was a wonderful feeling to walk down the street, long hair flying, wedge shoes clicking, feeling as though you belonged, were a part of it, the clubs, the bookshops, bombed-out St Anne's church, the scruffy old buildings with their mean doorways posting models for hire, Berwick Street market, the cafes and restaurants, the trees of Soho Square, the narrow streets linking the breadth of Soho. It was a time of transition for every one of us and the Theatre Girls' Club was the means.

These were some of the happiest months of my life. After a very short spell working at the bakery a few doors down from the club, then in the back office of an Oxford Street fashion store (days endured in respective basements) there followed two weeks in Folkestone with Arthur Brough's rep company. Thereafter, a few months at the Vaudeville Theatre as Mary Land's understudy during the last year of the long-running *The Man Most Likely To*. My time at the Theatre Girls' Club is also marked by the songs I wrote in the basement (again) at 59 Greek Street. The basement ran the length of the dining room and kitchen above, and you got to it by stairs descending from the hallway. There, against the west wall, alone and battered, was an upright piano. The grand piano in the club room, two floors up, was no use to me being so public, so it was at the battered old upright in the basement that I sat, writing; the same piano which had served those earlier theatre girls although I didn't know it then.

I did know that some residents escaped into the night from our dormitory. One whose bed was directly across from mine – she was seventeen or so years old and wore hair-pieces, pink, two at a time, one upon the other – would put on a mini fur coat over her baby-doll pyjamas and disappear at about 11 pm to see her boyfriend who was connected to one of the Soho night clubs. She thought he loved her. I hope he did. We slept well, even though music from the three or four Greek Street strip clubs nearest to us competed with each other from early evening until early morning.

59 Greek Street had large windows at its front which let in a lot of light. On each floor were corridors which ran, north to south, between

the front and back rooms and which had never seen daylight. They had missed the 1965 renovations and felt distinctly Victorian. They had atmosphere. The building's glory was its staircase leading up from the hallway. This piece of internal architecture was beautiful. When, in the late 1990s I stood on Greek Street and knocked on the familiar double front doors, they were opened not by the ghost of Miss Bell but by a young man who told me the place was a refuge for men. It was then I glimpsed the hallway where the staircase had been and was no more.

It was another twenty years before Deborah and I entered the building. We went with Euan Barr of Soho Housing Association on a sunny day in April 2018 to see how the redevelopment was going. Standing in the living area of a newly constructed second floor apartment in the exact place my bed had been fifty years earlier, I looked again across to the top storeys of the buildings on the far side of Greek Street. Just for a moment, the dreams of the eighteen-year-old I once had been came back. Deborah visited her old room at the back of the building and I went down to say hello to the basement and to assure it that it once had been a creative space.

I do believe that most of us who stayed at 59 Greek Street, when it was the Theatre Girls' Club, gained from the experience. It was our own: a secure place in an insecure world, a place where we could relax and which is surely something every one of us needs in any age. I raise my glass to it. And again. And again.

NOTES

1. British History online http://www.british-history.ac.uk/survey-london/vols33-4/pp170-90. Greek Street was laid out in the second-half of the 1600s in the Parish of St Anne's when Oxford Street was known as Tiborn Street, and Soho Square as Kings Square. Two empty plots where Nos 59 and 60 Greek Street now stand were, until 1691, part of the curtilage of 27 Soho Square (built in the late 1600s by the Duke of Monmouth). It is possible that the plot occupied by No 59 contained no building at all until William Bradshaw raised warehousing there in the mid-1700s, which would make it one of the last buildings to be raised on Greek Street.

2. *The Times* 17 Jan 1855; 18 April 1858; 22 Dec 1871; 15 Jan 1872. A brief description of the original building is found in records at Westminster Archives, St Anne's Parish records, Particulars of sale of 59 Greek Street (1820), Finding No: 0463.

3. Humphreys R., 'Beginnings of the London Charity Organization Society' in *Poor Relief and Charity 1869–1945* (2001) Palgrave Macmillan, London. Roberts, Michael, J.D., *Charity Disestablished? The Origins of the Charity Organisation Society Revisited, 1868-1871*, Journal of Ecclesiastical History, Vol. 54, No. 1, January 2003.

4. *The Times* 1872 and 14 December 1875.

5. Smith, Mark K, *Maude Stanley, girls' clubs and district visiting* (2012) https://infed.org/mobi/maude-stanley-girls-clubs-and-district-visiting/

6. Sutherland, Gillian (2004). *"Stanley, Henrietta Maria, Lady Stanley of Alderley (1807–1895)"*. Oxford Dictionary of National Biography. Oxford University Press.

7. Perkin, Joan, *Victorian Women*, John Murray, (1993) p. 213; Russell, Bertrand, *Autobiography*, Routledge (p. 30). Bertrand Russell was the son of Katherine Louisa Russell and her husband John Russell, Viscount Amberley.

8. Algernon left the Anglican church in 1879 to be received into the Roman Catholic church by Cardinal Manning. He was appointed Auxiliary Bishop of Westminster in 1903.

9. *Birmingham Daily Post,* 6 Feb 1880, 'London Gossip'

10. *The Builder* (1882) Ref: 43 6070-2082 at the British Library, p.517.

11. Stanley, Maude, *Work About the Five Dials* (1878) p. 17. *See also* Stanley, Maud *Clubs for Working Girls,* (1890) in Booton, Frank (ed)

Studies in Social Education, Vol 1 1860-1890, Benfield Press (1985) p.118.

12.   Stanley, Maud *Clubs for Working Girls,* (1890) in Booton, Frank (ed) *Studies in Social Education, Vol 1 1860-1890*, Benfield Press (1985) p. 93.

13.   'Soho Working Girls Club & Home' GLC/AR/BR/07/1347 held at London Metropolitan Archives.

14.   Stanley, Maud *Clubs for Working Girls,* (1890) in Booton, Frank (ed) *Studies in Social Education, Vol 1 1860-1890*, Benfield Press (1985) p. 62.

15.   Stanley, Maud, *Work About the Five Dials* (1878) p. 22.

16.   'London Gossip' *Birmingham Daily Post,* 6 Feb 1880.

17.   *The Stage* 1 June 1883.

18.   'Soho Club for Working Girls' *Lloyd's Weekly Newspaper*, 4 November 1883

19.   Stanley, Maud *Clubs for Working Girls,* (1890) in Booton, Frank (ed) *Studies in Social Education, Vol 1 1860-1890*, Benfield Press (1985) p. 131.

20.   Stanley, Maud *Clubs for Working Girls,* (1890) in Booton, Frank (ed) *Studies in Social Education, Vol 1 1860-1890*, Benfield Press (1985) pp. 132, 134

21.   Westminster Archives, 'Board of Guardians' 1882-7/3/1889 A2229; *The Northern-Easter Daily Gazette* 'Raid on a Betting Club' 17 April 1890; *The Illustrated Police News* 26 April 1890.

22.   *Daily News,* 22 June 1886, 'Raid on a West-End Club'

23.   *The Courier and Argus* 18 Oct 1906 'London Pests'

24.   *The Times* 'Metropolitan Police Commission' 18 Oct 1906 and 21 Nov 1906; *Manchester Courier and Lancashire General Advertiser* 'Police and Public' 17 Oct 1906

25.   Stanley, Maud *Clubs for Working Girls,* (1890) in Booton, Frank (ed) *Studies in Social Education, Vol 1 1860-1890*, Benfield Press (1985) p. 104.

26.   Stanley, Maud *Clubs for Working Girls,* (1890) in Booton, Frank (ed) *Studies in Social Education, Vol 1 1860-1890*, Benfield Press (1985) p. 51.

27.   Stanley, Maud *Clubs for Working Girls,* (1890) in Booton, Frank (ed) *Studies in Social Education, Vol 1 1860-1890*, Benfield Press (1985) pp. 53, 119

28.   Petersen, W., *Malthus,* p.55

29.   Malthus, *An Essay on the Principle of Population,* (1798), p. 4. http://www.esp.org/books/malthus/population/malthus.pdf Malthus is referring here to Rousseau, Godwin and Condorcet.

30. Malthus, *An Essay on the Principle of Population,* (1798), p. 44

31. Malthus, *An Essay on the Principle of Population,* (1798), p. 42. Malthus wrote: 'To remove the wants of the lower classes of society is indeed an arduous task. The truth is that the pressure of distress on this part of a community is an evil so deeply seated that no human ingenuity can reach it. Were I to propose a palliative, and palliatives are all that the nature of the case will admit, it should be, in the first place, the total abolition of all present parish-laws. This would at any rate give liberty and freedom of action to the peasantry of England, which they can hardly be said to possess at present.' (p. 30)

32. Malthus *An Essay on the Principle of Population,* (1798), pp. 8-9; see also pp. 20-21,

33. Stanley, Maude *Clubs for Working Girls,* (1890) in Booton, Frank (ed) *Studies in Social Education, Vol 1 1860-1890,* Benfield Press (1985) p. 121. Maude Stanley came from a ten child family.

34. Malthus *An Essay on the Principle of Population,* (1798), pp. 8-9; see also p. 34,

35. Stanley, Maude *Clubs for Working Girls,* (1890) in Booton, Frank (ed) *Studies in Social Education, Vol 1 1860-1890,* Benfield Press (1985) p. 51.

36. Ruskin, John *Sesame and Lilies* Lecture II. Lilies. Of Queens' Gardens. Available through http://www.gutenberg.org/files/1293/1293-h/1293-h.htm#citation25

37. Stanley, Maude *Clubs for Working Girls,* (1890) in Booton, Frank (ed) *Studies in Social Education, Vol 1 1860-1890,* Benfield Press (1985) p. 63.

38. Stanley, Maude *Clubs for Working Girls,* (1890) in Booton, Frank (ed) *Studies in Social Education, Vol 1 1860-1890,* Benfield Press (1985) p. 57.

39. Stanley, Maude (1890) p.123.

40. DSA191 part 2, Chester Archives, letter written by Maude Stanley dated Feb 9, 1909(?) Presumably Fanny Burney's *Cecilia* written in 1782.

41. 1911 Census Enumerators' Books.

42. DSA 176, a letter from Etta [Macy?], undated, probably 1905, held at Chester Archives.

43. A list of affiliated clubs in 1890 appears in Booton, Frank (ed), *Studies in Social Education, Vol 1 1860-1890,* Benfield Press (1985)

44. THM 211/1/4 1952

45. THM 211/1/4/ 1953

46. Collins L.J. *Theatre at War 1914-18* Macmillan Press (1998) p.52.

47. *The Times* 19 June 1918.

48.   *Manchester Courier* 5 Dec 1914, 'Mrs E Compton's Home'; *The People* 24 January 1915, 'The Theatre Girls' Club'.

49.   Lawrence, Gertrude, *A Star Danced*, online transcription Project Gutenberg Australia, unpaged: http://gutenberg.net.au/ebooks07/0700891h.html#chapter1

50.   Morley, Sheridan, *Gertrude Lawrence* McGraw-Hill (1981) p. 18.

51.   Lawrence, Gertrude, *A Star Danced* online transcription Project Gutenberg Australia, Chapter 4 (unpaged)

52.   For the West Central Jewish Club and Settlement: https://infed.org/mobi/lily-montagu-girls-work-and-youth-work/ For the Three Acts Club: *London's West End Actresses and the Origins of Celebrity Charity* pp. 112-16.   The Rehearsal Club was founded in 1892 with a view to furnishing a quiet retreat 'for the girls who take "smaller parts" in the theatrical productions, during rehearsals and between afternoon and evening performances'. It was a popular club, 15,907 visits were logged in 1915 (*The Times* 12/4/1916) The Dictionary of British Women's Organizations, 1825-1960 is an excellent source of women's clubs. The Theatrical Ladies Guild, formed in 1891 by the actor Kitty Carson, also continued to raise funds for needy theatre workers.

53.   Hall Caine, T. H., *Our Girls* Hutchinson (1916) p.44

54.   *The Times* 14 Sept 1916 'The Primate's Call'; *The Times* 29 November 1916;   Bishop of London, Arthur Winnington-Ingram, was publicly criticised in 1916, the year of the Mission of Repentance and Hope, when he supported the action of an English trawler skipper who left survivors of a downed German zeppelin to drown in the waters off the British coast. The skipper's actions were justified, the bishop said, because the chivalry of war had been 'killed by the Germans, and their word could not be trusted.' (*The Times* 7 February 1916 'The Trawler and the L19';   *Daily Gazette for Middlesborough* 8 Feb 1816 'Reprisals and Chivalry') The bishop said that Britain must stand as a 'pillar of strength' before other countries; she must emerge from the war purer than when she went in. This national purity was the fundamental hope and aim of that year's Mission of Repentance and Hope. Unsurprisingly, many were appalled by the Bishop of London's stance.

55.   Williams, Gordon, *British Theatre in the Great War,* Continuum (2003) pp. 24, 109, 110.

56.   *Nottingham Journal* 1 Jan 1915; *Central Somerset Gazette* 1 Jan 1915

57.   *The National Mission of Repentance and Hope,* Society of Promotiong Christian Knowledge (1919).

58.   THM 211/1/4 Annual Reports.

59. *Coventry Evening Telegraph* 13 April 1937.
60. Mackenzie *Octavo One* pp. 19-20, 31, 138, 15
61. THM 211/1/4
62. *Daily Herald* 6 May 1940.
63. *The Times* 19 June 1918; THM. 211/2/1/ Subseries.
64. *The Times* 5 February 1919 'King's Bench Division'
65. Compton Mackenzie, *Octave Five* p. 182; Compton Mackenzie, *Octave Three* p.67
66. Mukerji,   Jenny,
    ttps://www.surreyinthegreatwar.org.uk/story/pineroyd-letter-case-industry/
67. *The Times* 15 March 1920.
68. Hansard *19 February 1919 vol 112 cc939*
69. 'Report on British servants' *Bristol Evening News* 19 Feb 1919, quoted in Marwick, A. & W. Simpson, *War, Peace and Social Change: Europe 1900-1955 Documents 1: 1900-1929* p. 90
70. Marwick, Arthur, *War, Peace and Social Change 1900-1967*, Pelican (1970) p. 46.
71. Billy Hill, quoted in Morton, James, *Gangland,* Piatkus (2008) p.59
72. Morton, James, *Gangland,* Piatkus (2008) 39-41.
73. *The Times* 14 May 1920; *The Times* 13 May 1921
74. *The Times* 15 May 1923
75. *Dundee Courier* 19 Dec 1928
76. *The Times* 30 March 1921; THM 211/1/2/2/ (1970/A/87)
77. THM 211/1/2/2/ (1970A/87 Minute Book 1, July 22-Feb 28)
78. *The Times* 19 February 1923
79. Compton Mackenzie, *Octave Five* p.205.
80. THM211/1/2/1
81. Compton Mackenzie, *Octave Five* p.193; *Nottingham Evening Post* 23 July 1923.
82. THM 211/1/2/2/ Minutes No. 1, 8 Oct 1924 meeting.
83. *ibid.* Joint Electricity Authorities, effectively a nationalised service, were set-up through the Electricity Supply Act (1919) which was when homes began to benefit from this provision.
84. THM 211/1/2/2/ Minutes No. 1, 18 Dec 1924. Ethel Henry Bird's name appears in the Musicians' Chapel Book of Remembrance, St. Sepulchre-without-Newgate.
85. THM 211/1/2/2/ Minutes No. 1, 8 Oct 1924 meeting.
86. Compton Mackenzie *My Life and Times*, *Octave Six* p. 67.
87. *Coventry Evening Telegraph* 13 April 1937.
88. THM 211/1/2/1/
89. *ibid*

90. *Belfast Telegraph*, 30 Sept 1925.
91. *Nottingham Evening Post* 30 Sept 1925.
92. Perkin, Joan, *Victorian Women,* John Murray, (1993) p. 233; *North London News*, 14 Nov 1985.
93. McConnell, Marilyn, documents held by the author, to be submitted to the V&A Archives.
94. Probert, Rebecca, 'The controversy of equality and the Matrimonial Causes Act of 1923', https://heinonline.org.
95. Women's Library Archive website https://archiveshub.jisc.ac.uk/search/archives/a97a5bcd-eb99-31df-b564-8e75a4c33fb7
96. *Dundee Courier* 19 Dec 1928.   Early members of the National Vigilance Association included Mrs Fawcett, Mrs Percy Bunting, J Stansfeld MP, W. T. Stead, Ellice Hopkins, Mrs Mitchell, Mrs Lynch, Miss Bewicke, Mrs Bradley and Josephine Butler. Before the turn of the century the National Vigilance Association had established the International Bureau of the Suppression of the White Slave Traffic. The Jewish Association for the Protection of Women and Girls started out as the Jewish Ladies' Society for Preventive and Rescue Work. Both associations had been founded in 1885 in direct response to W. T. Stead's initiative.
97. Morton, James, *Gangland Soho*, Piatkus Books (2008) p. 51.
98. *The Scotsman* 19 Dec 1928.
99. *Birmingham Daily Gazette* 30 Jan 1929. Goddard's corrupt activities extended beyond Greek Street. He was also taking bribes from the owners of the 43 Club on Gerrard Street, and Murrays on Beak Street; *see* Morton, James, *Gangland Soho*, Piatkus Books (2008) pp. 52-3.
100. THM 211/1/2/2 Minutes No 1
101. Royal Opera House website: https://www.roh.org.uk/people/ninette-de-valois
102. THM 211/1/2/2 Minutes No 1
103. *Sunday Independent (Dublin)* 17 July 2005.
104. THM 211/1/2/1; THM 211/1/4/ [1939].
105. THM 211/1/2/1/
106. *The Times,* 5 Sept 1907.
107. Correspondence held by the author from Jill Shapiro, former Windmill Girl, and from Joan Beretta on behalf of Mike Hutton, author of *Story of Soho.*
108. *Sunday Tribune* 14 April 2002.
109. Hutton, Mike, *The Story of Soho,* Amberley (2013) p.17

110. Rhoda Anakaret L'Estrange married Charles James Stanley Howard, 10th Earl of Carlisle, son of Maude Stanley's sister Rosalind Frances. Members of the Council of Girls' Clubs Union at this time were Michael Furse, Bishop of St Albans; the Rev. Pat McCormick of St Martin's Place; Rhoda, Countess of Carlile; Lilian Bayliss, manager of the Old Vic; actress Rose Bishop; Vane Weatherston; publisher Gerald Duckworth; Nancy Greene; Jessie Moreshead a social worker; Constance Rivington; actors Lady Maud Tree, Sybil Thorndyke and Cyril Maud; and the Revs. Donald Hole and Evelyn Kingsbury both of the Actors' Church Union. (THM 211/1/3/7 First Memorandum)
111. Compton Mackenzie, *Octave Three* p.39.
112. THM 211/2
113. THM 211/1/3/7 First Memorandum.
114. THM 211/2/1
115. Morton, James, *Gangland Soho*, Piatkus Books (2008) pp. 75-80.
116. *Coventry Evening Telegraph* 13 April 1937.
117. *Ibid*
118. Compton Mackenzie, *Octavo Three* p. 43; *Illustrated London News* 1 October 1971; *Illustrated London News* 25 April 1970; *Daily Mirror* 28 December 1970.
119. Compton Mackenzie, *Octave Three* p.255.
120. THM 211/1/4/ 'Report for 1939'.
121. THM 211/2/1
122. *Ibid*
123. *The Times*, 10 Dec 1939.
124. TMH 211/1/4/
125. *Ibid*
126. THM 211/2/1
127. Margaret Wilson email correspondence 29 May 2020 held by the author.
128. Calendar of Confirmations and Inventories, Scotland (1882 volume; 1932 volume); 1901 English census. The Bell family was researched by Tom Barclay and Sheena Crook of The Local History Department, Carnegie Library, 12 Main Street, Ayr.
129. THM 211/1/4/ (1944).
130. *The Tatler* 5 Sept 1945.
131. THM 211/1/4/ (1944).
132. GL/AR/BR/07/1347 Soho Working Girls' Club & Home, 57 [*sic*] Greek Street, Case No: 1347, held at the London Metropolitan Archives.
133. THM 122/2/1.
134. *The Tatler* 5 Sept 1945.

135. *Daily Herald* 16 April 1941.
136. *Daily Herald* 26 March 1941.
137. *Daily Herald* 12 August 1941.
138. *Daily Mirror* 12/2/42; *see also* Morton, James, *Gangland Soho*, Piatkus Books (2008) p. 101.
139. THM 211/2/1.
140. THM 211/1/4/ [1944]
141. *Ibid*
142. *Daily Mirror* 10 November 1943.
143. de Beauvoir, Simone, from *The Second Sex* quoted in Marwick, A & W Simpson, *War, Peace and Social Change: Europe 1900-1955 Documents 2: 1925-1959* Open University Press (1999) p. 167.
144. THM 211/1/4/ [1944].
145. THM 211/1/4
146. These are the recollections of those who stayed at the Theatre Girls' Club from the 1940s to the 1960s and who generously responded to an appeal Deborah Lavin and I made through the pages of the British Actors' Equity Magazine in 2018. E-mail correspondence is held by the author who intends to offer it to the V&A Archives. Other recollections come from publications and newspapers as cited.
147. Telephone conversation between the author and Mary Wylie (2018).
148. Boothroyd, B. *Betty Boothroyd, The Autobiography,* Century (2001) pp. 20-22.
149. Barry, A., *It's not a Rehearsal*, Headline (2002) pp. 46, 48-9, 60-61, 64-6, 68, 83-4. Reference to the club's telephone number comes from a letter held in THM 211/2/1. In my time (1968-70) the public telephone was in the hallway and there was another half way up the stairs leading from the south-west corner of the club room, probably on the second floor, at the corridor's south end.
150. Vermer, Doremy, in Boothroyd, Betty, *The Autobiography*, Century (2001) pp. 22-3.
151. *Kensington Post* 27 March 1948.
152. Bruce Boyce (1910-1996) settled in London in 1946. His first performances were as a concert singer, for which he seems to have been best known. He also recorded. From 1956 he worked as a professor at the Royal Academy of Music.
153. Cox, P, *Gender, Justice and Welfare in Britain, 1900-1950: Bad Girls in Britain, 1900-1950*, p. 58
154. *Daily Herald* 18 July 1950
155. In the 1940s Rosemary Carter worked as a stage manager for Derek Salsberg's touring pantomime productions. She had hoped to continue as stage manager with Salsberg's Wolverhampton repertory

company but was thought too young to cope with the demands of weekly rep. When she married she gave up her career because, she said, she couldn't work in the theatre and be a housewife and mother. (Telephone conversation between the author and Rosemary Carter)

156. Derek Hunt in the *Soho Clarion,* issue 116 p. 6, The Soho Society
157. *The Stage* 5 March 1953
158. THM211/1/4 Annual Reports 1939
159. email held by the author (2021)
160. email held by the author (2021)
161. Barry, A., *It's not a Rehearsal*, Headline (2002) p. 84. Winston's nightclub was on Clifford Street, where 'dancing partners were available', so there was an obvious three-tier hierarchy of women performers: strippers, hostesses and revue dancers. (https://www.pinterest.co.uk/pin/332210909990958560)
162. notes made by author during a telephone conversation with Mary Wylie (2018)
163. *Soho Guide* 1951: p. 120
164. *Truth* 4 May 1956, *Daily Herald* 14 July 1958
165. http://www.sohomemories.org.uk/page/the_interval_club-pamela_anderson
166. The Wolfenden Report. https://sti.bmj.com/content/sextrans/33/4/205.full.pdf
167. https://www.legislation.gov.uk/ukpga/Eliz2/7-8/57/section/1
168. Barry, A., *It's not a Rehearsal*, Headline (2002) p. 66
169. Morton, James, *Gangland Soho,* Piatkus (2008) p. 212
170. for Harrison Marks *see* Hutton, Mike, *The Story of Soho,* Amberley (2013), pp.140-42
171. *Birmingham Daily Post* 28th Oct 1957
172. *Kensington Post* 16 July 1987
173. Wendy Cook, quoted on Darkest London website, https://darkestlondon.com/tag/club-tropicana/
174. *Sunday Tribune*, 14 April 2002.
175. *The Times* 20 Sept 2020
176. In 1970 an unmarried nineteen year old, Mary, pregnant and whose parents rejected her and for whom society did little, told her story from a woman's refuge: 'I was three months pregnant when my parents found out . . . I had to go to hospital for an operation [and] a young nurse told my mother because there were a few complications during the operation because I was pregnant. My father came storming into me just before the operation and went hammer and tongs at me. My mother was just as mad. I really wanted the child. My boyfriend John suggested an abortion but I wasn't very keen. He

got me into this hostel... I couldn't bring [David the baby] here...I worked in a supermarket and my wages were £7...this wasn't enough ...I couldn't have got a flat for much under £4 a week, and then I would have to pay someone to look after David all day. [The Children's Department found him a foster home.] I have shut him out of my life now. But I shall always remember than I have a son somewhere.' [*Middlesex County Times* 13 Nov 1970]

177. Anna Pollak (1912-1996) was a mezzo-soprano who stayed at the Theatre Girls' Club in the 1930s, probably at the time she was working as an actor in repertory and as a singer in theatre and revue. She toured with E.N.S.A during the war, and when peace came she joined Sadlers Wells Opera Company, also the English Opera Group. She received an OBE in 1962.

178. Mary Wylie visited Agnes Bell in Troon. (Telephone conversation between Mary Wylie and the author, 2018)

179. Charity Commission Number 205694

180. email received by the author from Marilyn Rogers

181. *The Stage* 7 July 1966

182. Russell, Bertrand, *Autobiography*, Routledge, p.81

183. email correspondence between Deborah Lavin and the author 2018

184. Morton, James, *Gangland,* Piatkus (2008) p. 154

185. *Daily Mirror* 5 Dec 1972; *The Stage* 7 Dec 1972. Compton Mackenzie died on 30 Nov 1972 in Edinburgh and was buried on the Isle of Barra.

186. *Kensington Post* 7 Aug 1970; Hansard, 16 April 1973 'Accommodation for the Homeless Young'.

187. *Illustrated London News* 22 Aug 1970

188. Humphreys, R. *Poor Relief and Charity 1869-1945.*

189. AST 36/674 (20A). Details on Christian Action's tenure of 59 Greek Street are taken from documents held at the National Archives, Kew: Ministry of Social Security, ' Vagrancy: Theatre Girls' Club, AST 36 1405 and AST 36/674

190. AST 36/1405, unnumbered documents pinned to front of file.

191. Brandon, David, *Homeless*, Sheldon Press (1974) p. 31. David Brandon (1941-2001) had experienced homelessness as a boy in the 1950s. As a young man he worked as a psychiatric social worker in local government and for a while was Consultative Social Services Advisor for Christian Action (*Acton Gazette* 17 June 1971). He also acted as research advisor for Jeremy Sandford's *Cathy Come Home.*

192. Brandon, David, *Homeless*, Sheldon Press (1974) p. 17

193. Brandon, David, *Homeless*, Sheldon Press (1974) p. 32. What Ursula Peters did after her four years at 59 Greek Street has not, so

far, been traced. It is possible that the registered death at Slough for one Ursula Berta E. Peter in the first quarter of 1981, (Ref: 19 0658) refers to our Ursula Peters.

194. Brandon, David, *Homeless*, Sheldon Press (1974) p. 14
195. Brandon, David, *Homeless*, Sheldon Press (1974) p. 34
196. Brandon, David, *Homeless*, Sheldon Press (1974) pp. 81-2
197. Brandon, David, *Homeless*, Sheldon Press (1974) p. 108
198. *Social Work Today* Vol 4, No 6, 14 June 1973
199. AST 36/1405 (71A II)
200. *Suggs and the City,* Headline (2009) p. 20
201. AST 36/1405 (55A)
202. Theatre Girls' Club management committee members were Elizabeth Bayliss (ex TGC worker), Christopher Brooke-Smith (ex-TGC worker), Christine Holloway from Consortium, Doris Harle, Peter Barnes (Home Office Probation Officer), John Previtt (consultant actuary); R. Blackwell (Supplementary Benefits Commission – non-voting observer)   Their solicitor was Richard Bowman. (AST 36/1405 (86A)
203. *Time Out* (no date given) https://www.timeout.com/movies/theatre-girls
204. AST 36/1405: (71A II, 72A)
205. AST 36/1405: (88B) for Thompson's comments; (58A) for Austerberry's comment
206. AST 36/1405: (71A II, 72A)
207. AST 36/1405: (87A)
208. AST 36/1405 (Homeless Action and Accommodation, Annual Report 1977-78)
209. AST 36/1405: (88C)
210. HO 383/412 (6C, 6D)

BIBLIOGRAPHY

Archives relating to 59 Greek Street are held by London Metropolitan Archives, under 'Soho Working Girls Club & Home' GLC/AR/BR/07/1347, and Westminster Archives, St Anne's Parish Records

The Stanley Family archive is held by Chester Archives, under DSA191

The Theatre Girls' Club archive is held by V&A Archive, London, under THM/211 sub-sections

Archives relating to Christian Action's reception centre at 59 Greek Street are held by the National Archives, Kew, Ministry of Social Security, ' Vagrancy: Theatre Girls' Club' under AST 36/1405 and AST 36/674

Publications

Barker, Clive 'Theatre and society: the Edwardian legacy, the First World War and the inter-war years', in Barker, C. and Maggie B Gale (eds) *British Theatre between the Wars, 1918-1939,* Cambridge University Press (2000)

Barrie, Amanda, *It's not a Rehearsal*, Headline (2002)

Boothroyd, Betty, *The Autobiography*, Century (2001)

Booton, Frank (ed) *Studies in Social Education, Vol 1 1860-1890*, Benfield Press (1985)

Brandon, David, *Homeless*, Sheldon Press, (1974)

The Builder (1882) Ref: 43 6070-2082 held at the British Library

Collins L.J., *Theatre at War 1914-18* Macmillan Press (1998)

Court, Percy G., *Memories of Show Business,* online:http://www.arthurlloyd.co.uk/MemoriesOfShowBusiness/Memories OfShowBusinessChapter4.htm

Hall Caine, *Our Girls,* Hutchinson (1916)

Kamieriski, Łukasz, *Shooting Up: A History of Drugs and War*, Hurst & Co. Publishers, online excerpt released with permission in the UK on 31st March 2016

Lawrence, Gertrude, *A Star Danced*, unpaged http://gutenberg.net.au/ebooks07/0700891h.html#chapter1

Mackenzie, Compton, *My Life and Times, Octave One* Chatto & Windus (1963); *Octave Three* (1964); *Octave Five* (1966); *Octave Six* (1967); *Octave Ten* (1971)

Malthus, Robert, *An Essay on the Principle of Population,* (1798)

Marwick, Arthur, *War, Peace and Social Change 1900-1967*, Pelican (1970)

Morley, Sheridan, *Gertrude Lawrence,* McGraw-Hill (1981)

Morton, James, *Gangland Soho,* Piatkus (2008)

Mukerji, Jenny, https://www.surreyinthegreatwar.org.uk/story/pineroyd-letter-case-industry/

Perkins. Joan, *Victorian Women,* John Murray, (1993)

Petersen, William, *Malthus,* Harvard College, Heinemann London, (1979)

Ruskin, John, *Sesame and Lilies* Lecture II. Lilies.

Russell, Bertrand, *Autobiography*, Routlege

Sandford, Jeremy, *Down and Out in Britain,* New English Library (1972)

Stanley, Maude, *Work About the Five Dials* (1878), held at the British Library

Stanley, Maude, *Clubs for Working Girls,* (1890), in Booton, Frank (ed) *Studies in Social Education, Vol 1 1860-1890*, Benfield Press (1985)

Suggs, *Suggs and the City*, Headline (2009)

Tames, Richard, *Soho Past*, Historical Publications (1994)

Williams, Gordon, *British Theatre in the Great War,* Continuum (2003)

INDEX

Index Note: subheadings listing biographical details are ordered chronologically. TGC refers to the Theatre Girls' Club.

160

Thorndyke, Sybil 27, 35, 36, 50
Thornton, Helene 93, 94
Three Arts Club 27
Tierney, Nessie 81
Tiller Girls 70, 72, 104, 115
Tiller School 71
Time Out 134
Toole, John Lawrence 9
Torchon, Elsie 53

Valentine, John 58
Van Damm, Vivian 49
Variety Artistes Federation 49
venereal disease 28
Vietnam War demonstrations 119

Ward, Nita 63
Wardour Street 5, 62, 63, 117
Webster, Ben 49
Webster, Vera 53-4
West Central Jewish Club and
    Settlement 26
Westminster City Council 60, 135-6
Westminster Jewish Girls' Club 6
Westminster Jews' Free School 3
Whatever Artists Management 118
'white sex trade' 40-41, 104
    vigilante watch-dogs 42-3
Whitty, May 49

Wilson, Margaret 75, 76-81
Windmill Theatre, *Revudeville* 49-50
Winnington-Ingram, Arthur, Bishop
    of London 28, 29, 31, 35, 55, 87,
    146
Wolfenden Report 89-90
women *see* gender discrimination
women's refuges 107, 129-30, 151-2
    see also reception for homeless
    women
working class poverty *see* class
    discrimination
World War I 24
    cocaine use 31
    National Union of Women
        Workers 28
    venereal disease, spread of 28
    West End theatres and 24, 27-8
    women's work 33-4
    Women's Emergency Corps 27
World War II 55-6
    bombing 59, 60-61, 64-5
    E.N.S.A. 63-4, 67, 74
    rationing 71, 74
Wylie, Mary 74-5, 76, 80
Wyndham, Charles 9

youth demonstrations (1968) 119
YWCA 77, 102, 116

Warm thanks go to Audrey Campbell, Maureen Miles, Margaret Wilson, Sheila Rennie, Helen Locke, Lois Daine, Jane Terry, Marilyn McConnell, Joy Clarkson, Carole Fripp, Jenny Dunster, Anabel Littledale and Carol Sagar for sharing their memories of their time at 59 Greek Street when it was the Theatre Girls' Club. Thanks also to Euan Barr of Soho Housing Association and to Sheena Crook and Tom Barclay of the Local History Department, Carnegie Library, Ayr, for so kindly providing Agnes Bell's family history details.

This is also in remembrance of Mary Wylie (27th July 1930 – 10th November 2019) whose recollections appear here.

Printed in Great Britain
by Amazon

30758673R00096